JOHANN WOLFGANG VON GOETHE

Torquato Tasso

Alan Brownjohn is the author of six volumes of verse and
his *Collected Poems 1952-83* is published by Secker &
Warburg. He has edited three verse anthologies,
including *First I Say This*, a selection of poetry for
speaking aloud (Hutchinson). He has been Chairman of
the Poetry Society since 1982.

T. J. Reed is a Fellow and Tutor in Modern Languages
at St John's College, Oxford. His books on German
literature include two studies of Goethe.

Also published by Angel Books:

Pushkin: *Mozart and Salieri: The Little Tragedies*
translated by Antony Wood

Fet: *I Have Come to You to Greet You: Selected Poems*
translated by James Greene
with essays by Henry Gifford and Yevgeny Vinokurov

M. Pavlović: *The Slavs beneath Parnassus: Selected Poems*
translated by Bernard Johnson

JOHANN WOLFGANG VON GOETHE

Torquato Tasso

A version by Alan Brownjohn
based on a literal translation by Sandy Brownjohn

Introduction by T. J. Reed

ANGEL BOOKS
LONDON

First published by Angel Books, 3 Kelross Road,
London N5 2QS

British Library Cataloguing in Publication Data
Goethe, Johann Wolfgang von
    Torquato Tasso.
    I. Title   II. Brownjohn, Alan
    III. Brownjohn, Sandy
    832'.6   PT2026.T7

    ISBN 0-946162-19-0

Typeset in Great Britain by Trintype,
printed by Nene Litho and bound by Woolnough Bookbinding,
all of Irthlingborough, Northants.

Contents

Torquato Tasso:
Born at Sorrento, 11 March 1544. Principal
work the chivalric epic *Gerusalemme Liberata*. At
various times in a wandering career, a
favourite at the court of the Estes at Ferrara;
but for seven years imprisoned by the Duke
after a fit of madness. Died in Rome, 25 April
1595.

Introduction

by T. J. Reed

> *Why, if thou never wast at Court, thou never*
> *saw'st good manners; if thou never saw'st*
> *good manners, then thy manners must be*
> *wicked; and wickedness is sin, and sin is*
> *damnation. Thou art in a parlous state,*
> *shepherd.*
>
> As You Like It, III, 2

When Goethe began writing *Torquato Tasso*, he had been five years a poet at a court himself, though not just a court poet. He was invited to Weimar in 1775 by the Duke, Carl August, who saw in the spectacular energies that had produced a brilliant historical drama (*Götz von Berlichingen*) and a sensational novel (*The Sufferings of Young Werther*) the promise of an equally energetic administrator for his small duchy. He was not alone in that. A friend of Goethe's had written the year before: 'Goethe would be a splendid man of action in the service of a prince . . . He has not just wisdom and affability, but vigour too.' Goethe was to spend the rest of his life in Weimar and make it the centre of modern German literary culture.

There were however initial disharmonies. Weimar scarcely welcomed this young protégé of the even younger Duke. To senior administrators he seemed an upstart queue-jumper, and sooner than help him from their fund of experience, they huffily threatened to resign. For the nobles at court, he was a bourgeois outsider who lacked decorum. Whatever his claims, as a poet of prodigious natural talent or as a man of remarkably compelling presence, he was a foreign body in their small world of convention – almost (as he later wrote) a kind of noble savage.

He established himself nevertheless, became a member of the Duchy's governing Council, and over the next ten years was entrusted (burdened, the writer came to feel) with the most varied responsibilities: roads, forests, mines, army recruitment, the exchequer. He also became accepted by the court, and more intimately (though still, it seems, platonically) by one court lady, Charlotte von Stein, who provided this often alarmingly impetuous poet with a finishing school in more moderate feeling and behaviour. But in 1786, frustrated by an excess of moderation and a decade of self-denial in the service of the community, he suddenly reasserted his personal creative destiny by escaping to Italy for two serene years of travel and study. It was there he returned to the Tasso project, left lying in the early 1780s like so many other works which his administrative duties edged out. The two-act fragment in prose became a verse-drama and was published in 1790.

The links between Goethe's private history and the play are obvious: the poet both dependent on and giving lustre to a small state, the outsider at court, etiquette versus impetuosity, art contrasted with practical affairs, the moderating influence of noble women, a platonic relationship. Goethe was always avowedly a poet of experience, and in old age he looked back on *Tasso* as 'flesh of my flesh and bone of my bone', and as a medium through which he had got the more painful of his Weimar experiences out of his system.

But just as obviously the play is not simple autobiographical confession. Tasso's vulnerability is greater, his practicality less, his capacity to generate social disharmony more extreme, than Goethe's. Even in its beginnings, the subject must have offered Goethe affinities rather than equivalence; and when he took it up again in 1788, he was an avowed classicist, aspiring beyond immediate self-expression to forms and statements of general validity. He now expressly discouraged the equation between Tasso in Ferrara and himself in Weimar.

So *Tasso* is best read as a more general study of The Poet, of the 'disproportion of talent and life', as Goethe said. It is given body by his knowledge of the historical Tasso (in the late stages of composition he drew on a new biography by Serassi) and quickened by personal reminiscence. The theme of 'the artist and society' has preoccupied modern writers, sometimes to the exclusion of substantive utterance on the world beyond their problems, but Goethe's has the distinction of being the first work in this now crowded category. He had no set character-stereotype to follow and no familiar plaints to echo. If the modern reader is struck most by Tasso's hypersensitivity and maladjustment, that is at least partly because later treatments of the theme have made these motifs standard. Goethe's text contains more, and more subtle, perceptions. Antedating as it does later attitudes of resignation, it makes a notable case for the poet – or, what is perhaps not quite the same thing, an incisive case against the social group that surrounds Tasso, differing from him radically, and determining his tragic or near-tragic fate. And in making this case, Goethe's play puts before us questions that are not peculiar to artists but concern the individual at large and his freedoms within the always restrictive structures of society.

These questions are expressly debated, as well as embodied, in the play. It opens with the Princess and Leonora Sanvitale dressed as shepherdesses, a pastoral pretence which recognises an ideal of 'nature', but stylises it into harmless unreality. It is no challenge to real society, but at best an escape from it – as it was for Marie-Antoinette at Versailles on the eve of the French Revolution, at precisely the time Goethe was writing. Then in the first scene of Act Two, Tasso and the Princess argue over the nature of the Golden Age, the ancient myth of the perfection society once had and might hope to find again. For Tasso, that ideal state would consist in freedom – 'You may do whatever brings delight' (line 994). He is not talking of political freedom (he expressly disavows any such aim and accepts his feudal subordination) but of a more fundamental spontaneity. For the Princess, it would lie in

the restraints of convention – 'You may do whatever things
are right' (line 1006). Shrewdly, Tasso answers: if only a
tribunal of noble people (he means inherently, not just
socially noble) could determine what the conventions
should be! As it is, the clever and the powerful manage to
enshrine as the social norm whatever suits their book.

This is not just shrewd, but also prophetic. Tasso is to be
first put in the wrong and then finally disqualified by the
rules of a group who are prepared to keep him while he
produces, praise him when he has produced, but not accept
him as he is – and certainly not adapt their ways to the
natural impulses by which he lives.

Not that he ever demands that they should, or refuses
obstinately to adapt himself to their requirements. It is at
the Princess's educative urging that he approaches Antonio
– only to get the rebuff which infuriates him into disgracing
himself. And if his heart-on-sleeve spontaneity is too brash
for the elder statesman to accept (though we learn later
how much pique and envy lay behind Antonio's façade of
fastidiousness), it is a spontaneous *humility*, an impetuous
quest for guidance from the more experienced, worldly
man. But instead, he receives intolerable provocation, from
an antagonist who never admits he is one, never infringes
the social rules in the way Tasso does by drawing his sword
within the palace precincts. While Tasso lays about him
with grand appeals to the free thought and noble feeling
which should be permitted everywhere, Antonio fights him
off with the rapier of convention. It is as much a duel as it
would be if they both had drawn. Antonio is transgressing
the rules even as he invokes them, for they were never
meant to allow such calculated insult. Tasso, shrewdly
again, says so, aptly repeating the key terms of the
Princess's social code: 'May I not do here what is right for
you?' (line 1346). The discreet persistence of such concepts
is what gives the play, at a deeper level than the interaction
of characters, its firm structure. In this brilliantly managed
quarrel-scene (II, 3), Tasso gives – allowing the radical
difference of viewpoint – as good as he gets.

But when the Duke enters to find him sword in hand,

Tasso inevitably seems to be in the wrong. It would take more sympathy than lies in Alfonso's capabilities or Antonio's interests to establish that, from Tasso's very different point of view, he was in the right. More sympathy, too, than many literary critics have been able to raise for Goethe's poet. Strangely, they often accept without question that Tasso is at fault for his lack of savoir vivre in the highly civilised setting of the court. They see the play as a kind of versified etiquette book, Castiglione's *Courtier* redone negatively as a tale of exemplary blunders, with Tasso's precarious state of mind and emotions as a further unlovable feature, for which too he is somehow to blame.

I call this a strange view for two reasons. The first is that we are dealing with drama, and drama is structured on the conflict of opposed elements. The spectator looks on from a standpoint outside either, he does not enter into the assumptions of the one about the other – not, at any rate, until the action has begun to justify particular sympathies. In *Torquato Tasso*, convention and spontaneity are the opposed elements. There is no call to see the whole action through court eyes just because it is played out at court, that is, on convention's home territory. That is part of the dramatic set-up, not a ground of our understanding of the play. And this would be true even if the court kept its own rules impeccably, and proved their preeminent value as a way of life.

But in fact what the spectator sees – and this is the second reason why it is strange to make Tasso a moral scapegoat and reduce the play to a critique of the wayward artist – is that he is at least as much sinned against as sinning. Courtly urbanity is not so superior after all. Antonio turns out to have acted from pique at Tasso's enjoyment of laurels and the ladies' favour. He admits too that he was letting go after the wearing self-control of his diplomatic mission. Worse, even after he has undertaken to help Tasso, he denigrates him to the Duke: he gives an account of Tasso's habits which cannot be taken as 'the truth' about Tasso's way of life precisely because it comes from such an unsympathetic reporter, and by this stage we must allow for bias. As for the Duke, he fails – and comes to see that he has failed – to administer even-handed justice. He commits the typical establishment sin of continuing to trust his familiar agent, even though that agent is one of the parties in a scandal to be investigated. He is guilty of a grave error of judgment in sending Tasso off to a room-arrest which is certain to ferment his sense of grievance into a positive persecution complex. And as a Renaissance patron who views men as usable possessions and now sees his investment in this one starting to pay off, he keeps tight hold of Tasso's *Jerusalem Liberated* on the pretext (and this is the one occasion when anyone on the court side invokes 'nature') that any further work on the poem will spoil its primal splendour.

Then Leonora: she is even more ruthlessly self-seeking as she tries to detach Tasso from the Princess he loves and become his new muse, to her own greater temporal and permanent glory. And finally the Princess herself: pure and genuine though she is, it is her attempt to educate Tasso towards 'normality' that sets him off on the downward track (as, again, she later sees); and for all her insistence on restraint as a social ideal, the words she speaks in their last scene together, to a Tasso now desperately in need of emotional support, are so ambiguous in their expression of Platonic intent – can she herself fully understand and control her own deepest impulses? – as to be positively misleading and to invite disaster.

It is not surprising that Tasso, who is kept offstage crucially in mid-drama while the others plan or plot what to do with or for him, sees more ill-will in these actions and attitudes than there really is. He is wrong on points of fact, and his obsessive suspicions approach the paranoid. But he is not wholly wrong in essence. It may be no one is deliberately conspiring against him, as he believes – on the contrary, by their own lights the others are trying to help him. Yet at a level deeper than any conscious intentions, their society virtually *is* a conspiracy against him and the way he would wish to live, love and create. Their refined manners are a superstructure shaped by, yet half-concealing their interests; there is no understanding for his needs and compulsions. Only very late does the Princess say 'We don't want anything you cannot be' (line 3237); and there is no sign that any of them is actually about to act on that liberal principle. Even when Antonio, recovered from his pique, comes to conciliate Tasso, there is – less openly than in the quarrel scene, but still clearly – the same opposition of convention and true feeling. For Antonio, all can be well again because he never let fall any word which technically offended Tasso's honour. But Tasso still feels the essential hurt which cannot be undone by technical arguments. It is hard to look on at all this, and still think of Tasso as a mere social and psychological misfit – hard not to feel that Goethe has transformed the well-known story of a 'mad' poet from within (transforming stories from within was Goethe's usual dramatic procedure). Tasso is a piece of nature in an anxiously trimmed garden, as Goethe himself had been. At very least he stands beside Molière's misanthropist Alceste as a man with a good case against society. And since we all in a sense have a case against society, and the Rousseauian dialectic between us and it is the very fabric of life, Goethe's *Torquato Tasso* stands in a much more important tradition than simply that of writers' writings about writers.

Of course, it remains a play about a specifically *artistic* individual. Some scenes, it has been acutely argued, show us Tasso's poetic imagination taking fire and beginning to create visions as he speaks. His isolation from court society is in part the isolation needed to reflect on his themes and practise his craft. And at the close, when he has lost for good his footing in Ferrara, it is poetry he has to fall back on for consolation. Antonio, once his enemy but now his support and adviser, seems (his speeches are short and cryptic) to be confirming him in what he is after the disasters others have caused by pressing him to be what he is not. He must know himself: 'You can try to recognise what you are!' (line 3420) – a doubly apt injunction, echoing the famous oracle of Apollo, the god of poetry and poets. Tasso must be fully and unashamedly a poet, with everything that entails. What nature offers in return is the gift of healing utterance where other men have only dumb pain – a boon to the poet himself before ever it is heard as 'literature' by other people. Writing has never been a source of doubt or suffering for Tasso as it was to be for later writers, real and fictive – he is miserable only when prevented from following his natural bent: 'And if I did not write, and think, poetry,/My life could not have the name of life' (lines 3081-2). Now in adversity, his gift becomes more vital to him than ever.

This final affirmation of poetry and of its intimate link with life comes not just from Tasso's but from Goethe's deepest feeling. It was the principle he lived by, through delight and distress, and in his last profound crisis the old poet was to recall Tasso's words – 'Where other men must suffer grief in silence,/A god gave me the power to speak my pain' (lines 3432-3) – and make his own salvation once more by turning emotional pain into the 'word and melody' of one of his greatest poems.

An apotheosis of poetry, then, as a man's desperate response to disaster. Yet when the healing utterance has performed its private function and eventually comes to be heard by others, it resumes the dialectic of individual and society on a new plane. For what nature gave the poet was only 'melody', the line of the lone voice that expresses his individual being, and it has to take its chance of being assimilated into a larger harmony among men – has to gain acceptance in the world where the poet himself in his angular uniqueness came to grief. But it has beauty and eloquence to help it: the human individuality that was so vulnerable has hardened into a new and strangely authoritative element.

The Verse of Goethe's *Torquato Tasso*

German writers took over Shakespearean iambic pentameter blank verse from the mid-eighteenth century onwards, as part of their conscious reshaping of German literature on English rather than French models. By 1790 it

was established as the standard form for serious drama and
– amazingly, after such a short period of practice – virtually
perfected as a poetic medium.

Appropriately for a play that treats social convention, the
blank verse of *Torquato Tasso* has an elegance and harmony
beyond anything to be found in Goethe's other dramas.
This is partly a matter of the smooth movement and
musicality of the lines – appropriately again, it is Tasso
himself who most noticeably, in moments of emotion,
breaks the bounds of metrical regularity; but it is also a
matter of intellectual control and of play with the concepts
that arise from the central issues. The characters are
constantly formulating near-epigrammatic statements of
their personal views, turning sentiments into *sententiae* –
maxims, general truths, social axioms. As a result, much of
the dialogue has a spacious, leisurely quality that exactly
suggests the quality of civilised life at the Este court, just as
the polish of individual statements suggests their unanswer-
able rightness. This may seem positively undramatic, but it
is the perfect expression of a stylised calm out of which the
drama bursts. And the epigrammatic style itself becomes
dramatic when statements are pared down to briefer and
briefer form, until at climaxes like the quarrel-scene both
speakers are finally compressing their anger and their
arguments into a sequence of finely-tempered single lines –
what the Greeks called 'stichomythia' – and the flickering
exchange of concepts embodies their underlying duel.

Though he works in Shakespeare's metre, Goethe
nowhere approaches Shakespeare's grand manner and
flamboyant imagery. The style is muted, befitting a
chamber-drama. I can think of no English equivalent for its
style of highly-charged restraint, precarious formality. A
literal translation of its 'sententious' tone would therefore
strike no familiar chord with an English audience, but
would probably sound stilted and pedantic. It needs to be
deformalised, eased out of its fixed verbal positions, while
keeping the underlying antitheses of attitude between the
characters clearly in view through a more contemporary
urbanity. This seems to me what Alan Brownjohn has
aimed at, and achieved.

TRANSLATORS' NOTE

Goethe's strong and lucid blank verse carries not only the
formality of the court of Ferrara but also the complex and
delicate responses of its inhabitants to the unpredictable
genius in their midst. In this version we have done our best
to retain the structure and length of speeches, and to reflect
as closely as possible the cast of Goethe's utterance. It
seemed important not to try to impose on the play, at will,
any alien style or arbitrary updating: its speeches are
powerful enough, and its consideration of the artist at odds
with his patrons 'modern' enough, not to require liberties to
be taken. Besides, the personal conflicts in this drama are
presented with unmistakable emotional force. *Torquato
Tasso* is not only great poetry; it is also highly-charged
conversation. The aim of this version is to combine these
qualities in an actable rendering suited to our own time and
acceptable to the ears of a modern audience.

A.B.
S.B.

Publisher's Note

Line-numbering indicates as closely as possible that of the
original text.

Torquato Tasso

CHARACTERS

Alfonso II, Duke of Ferrara
Leonora d'Este, sister of the Duke
Leonora Sanvitale, Countess of Scandiano
Torquato Tasso
Antonio Montecatino, Secretary of State

The scene: The palace of Belriguardo

ACT ONE

A garden terrace adorned with busts of the epic poets.
Downstage right is Virgil, downstage left is Ariosto.

SCENE 1

Princess; Leonora.

PRINCESS

Leonora, first you smile at me, and then
You appear to be smiling at yourself.
May a friend know what is on your mind
When you can seem so pleased – and yet so thoughtful?

LEONORA

No mystery! I felt pleased to see us both
Playing at being shepherdesses, dressed
In simple country clothes, weaving our garlands
– And then I realised that while I sat
Heaping up flower on flower in one mere mass
Of brilliant colours, you had twined your laurel   10
Into such very subtle shapes – the work
Of a much finer mind, and nobler heart.

PRINCESS

I did it without even thinking . . .
Still, now it's finished, I can see a head
Which is worthy of a crown. This can be Virgil's!

(She crowns the bust of Virgil.)

LEONORA

Then I shall set this full and happy garland
On the head of our most glorious master
Ariosto –

(She crowns the bust of Ariosto)
His light spirit is eternal,
And now he has his share of our own spring.

PRINCESS
It is kind of my brother to bring us out   20
To the country so soon. Here in Belriguardo
We can be alone, and for hours on end
Imagine this is the poets' golden age.
You know I lived here when I was young?
I was happy then . . . And days like this,
When the sun restores the green to the same land,
Give me that lost age back again.

LEONORA
Yes, this is a new world all around us!
The cool shade of these evergreens delights
Our hearts already, and the rushing sound   30
Of the waters in the fountain restores
Our spirits once again. The young branches sway
In the morning breeze, and the flowers gaze up
From the soil with the eyes of friendly children.
Already the gardener lifts the covers
From the house of the lemon and orange trees.
The deepest peace fills the blue sky above,
And on the horizon now the distant snow
Melts from the mountains in a gentle mist.

PRINCESS
I should welcome this spring without reserve   40
If I did not have to lose my friend –

LEONORA
Which means that you will spoil these lovely hours
Reminding me how soon I have to leave –

PRINCESS
– Though whatever pleasures you leave behind,
You will find twice the number in Florence.

LEONORA

You know that love and duty call me back:
My husband has been without me for so long
I must show him his son – who has grown so fast,
And learnt so fast this year, that I must return
And share in his father's joy. But as for Florence,   50
That is a great and marvellous place, and yet,
For all its accumulated treasures,
It cannot compare with Ferrara.
The people made our Florence what it is:
Ferrara gained its greatness through its princes.

PRINCESS

We owe much more to chance: some gifted people
Happened to meet here – and combined their talents.

LEONORA

But chance can scatter things so easily.
No – because you are noble, noble minds
Are attracted here, and once they have arrived   60
You have the skill to keep them. You and your brother
Do credit to your own great ancestors
By assembling minds that are worthy of you.
A free and independent human spirit
Flourished here from the start, like a strong, pure light
In a world of brutal darkness. Only think
Of those great names – Ippolito d'Este,
And Ercole d'Este! Such grand princes
Were my childhood heroes, and my father praised
Ferrara in the same breath as Florence,   70
Or even Rome. I often yearned to be
Where I am now, in the place where Petrarch
Was welcomed and encouraged, where Ariosto
Found models for his writing. – Can Italy
Tell you of any great name whom this house
Has not called its guest? And you sense how much
You gain by providing for a genius:
You are well aware that genius repays you
With enormously richer gifts, and hallows

The very ground you walk on, so when you die,   80
All the civilisation it has built
Survives you, and enriches your descendants.

PRINCESS

It would if those descendants were to show
Your enviable passion for such things.

LEONORA

But you have that passion too, and quite without
The brashness of others. Where I instantly
Parade all the things I feel so strongly,
You are feeling everything much more deeply,
And saying nothing. No passing glory
Ever affects you, you are not charmed   90
By facile wit – no one can flatter you.
Your mind is strong, and your fine judgement
Hardly ever falters. In your own greatness,
You recognise the great gifts of others.

PRINCESS

You should not make such use of true friendship
To flatter me in so extreme a way.

LEONORA

But friendship is the fairest of all things.
As your friend, I am in the best position
To judge all your merits. I am quite aware
That chance and opportunity do count,   100
But your culture is something you were born with:
The whole world honours you and your sister
As the oustanding women of the age.

PRINCESS

Such praise does not move me, Leonora.
Our gifts are very modest, and what we are
We owe mostly to others. If I know
The ancient tongues, and if I love the richest
Legacies of antiquity, I should thank

My mother. Lucretia and myself
Cannot match her intellect, though if you must have   110
One to compare with her, then take Lucretia.
I can assure you that I never thought
Rank or possessions gave me any right
To what I had from Nature, or through pure chance.
It delights me to know I can understand
What the scholars are discussing. It might be
A question of some figure from the past,
And the true worth of what he did; or perhaps
A conversation on some theory which,
If you put it to the test, might well inspire   120
And benefit a man – wherever
The talk of noble scholars leads I love
To follow, because I find it easy
To keep up with their clever arguments.
I love to listen when they calmly speak
Of all those powerful forces which may seem
Agreeable, yet have the strength to shake
Men's souls to their foundations; I am absorbed
When someone starts a discourse on why great princes   130
Should long to be even more rich and famous;
And when the gift of knowledge is employed
To enlighten us rather than to deceive –

LEONORA

And when these serious discussions stop,
We relax both our intellect and our ears
With the easier pleasures of poetry,
The art which harmonises all the things
Philosophy leaves in discord! Yours
Is a rare spirit which takes in the wide
Realm of all learning – I prefer to stay   140
With poetry, here in these groves of laurel.

PRINCESS

Yet they say the tree that flourishes here
More than any other, is the myrtle
– Which is Venus's tree! And although we have

Many Muses to pick from, we hardly look
To them for a friend, or companion,
We look to the poet. So it makes me sad
That ours often seems to avoid us,
Or even run away, in his long pursuit
Of something we cannot know about, and he   150
May not even know himself. It would be pleasant
If he met us at some fortunate hour
And suddenly saw that *we* were the treasure
He had found nowhere else in the world.

LEONORA

There was a little truth in your first words,
And your joke is not one to offend me . . .
I *am* fond of Tasso, which is natural
In someone who honours all men's talents.
But yes – our world might not exist for him:
He listens to the harmonies of nature,   160
And his mind is constantly absorbing all
That history and human life can yield him.
He has the sort of intellect that turns
Sheer chaos into order, and even breathes
Life into dead things. Whatever seems
Most ordinary to us he can at once
Change into wonders, while what we cherish
Means little to him. He is wonderful –
He walks in his own magic world, and draws
Other people in to share it – yet when   170
He seems to come close, he is still far away:
For him we could be disembodied spirits.

PRINCESS

You capture him so well – and tenderly –
This poet hovering among his dreams;
But I sense that the real world does attract him,
And draw him just as strongly. When he writes out
His love songs, and fixes the manuscripts
To the trees in this garden, giving us
A new Hesperides, where poems take

The place of golden apples – aren't all those   180
The fruits of a true and earthly love?

LEONORA
I have seen those too . . . and admire them.
But have you noticed how his various rhymes
All praise one image in particular?
Now he lifts it up to the starry heavens,
And worships it as angels will adore
Their god above the clouds; then he follows it
Through silent fields where every flower he finds
Is twined into a garland. And if ever
The one he honours goes away, he dotes on   190
The very ground that her foot has travelled,
And hides away like a nightingale, filling
This grove and all the air with the sweet lament
Of a lovesick heart. Such harmonies
Of plaintive grief and longing would enthral
Any ear that heard them –

PRINCESS
          – And of course,
If you asked him to name that image,
He would call it – 'Leonora'.

LEONORA
But your own name is Leonora too:
If it were not so, then I should resent it.   200
I am pleased he should want to hide his feelings
In a double meaning, and not disclose
That he really means you; and quite content
If he chooses also to remember me
With the gracious sound of this one name.
The question here is not that of a love
Which strives to overcome, and to possess
For its own jealous satisfaction; while
He glories in the happy contemplation
Of your own great merits, he might also find   210
Some lighter things in me to entertain him.

Tasso is not 'in love' with us – if you
Forgive my saying that. He combines
In this one name we have, all his ideal
Visions of things, and shares them with us.
If we seem to love the man, we are only
Loving, with him, the highest we can love.

PRINCESS

You have explored this whole philosophy
More deeply than I thought, Leonora . . .
You tell me things my ear may understand –   220
But my soul finds it hard to admit them.

LEONORA

You have sat at Plato's feet! How can it be
That a beginner's arguments could puzzle
A scholar like yourself? It could just be
That I have been very much mistaken –
But I honestly don't think I am.
Love never appears in Plato's teachings
As the spoilt child he used to be: this Love
Is the youth who married Psyche, with a place
In the council of the gods, and not that Love   230
Who raged on, wantonly, from heart to heart
And pounced on any beauty, only to find
He had to suffer, for these hasty pleasures,
All the pains of anger and disgust.

PRINCESS

Leonora, my brother is coming! Please,
Don't mention this conversation, or else
We shall have to face more of the teasing
He gave us about our dresses.

(Enter Alfonso.)

SCENE 2

Princess; Leonora; Alfonso.

ALFONSO

I've been looking everywhere for Tasso,
And don't even find him here with you.   240
Would you happen to know where he might be?

PRINCESS

I've hardly seen him for the past two days.

ALFONSO

This is one of his oldest failings,
This hiding himself away. I understand
If he prefers the company of his thoughts
And chooses not to mix with the crowd.
But I don't approve of that if it means
He contrives to avoid the very friends
Who value him most profoundly.

LEONORA
                    If, my lord,   250
You wait a little longer, you may change
Your reproaches into cries of gratitude.
I saw him – from a distance – this very day.
He was clutching his book and his writing slate,
And pacing up and down; from time to time
He would stop and alter something. Last night
He gave a hint that it might be complete:
With a few last revisions he will have
An offering worthy of all your kindness.

ALFONSO

When he does bring it I shall make him welcome,
And release him from any obligations   260
For a long time ahead. I take great interest
In all he writes, and in particular
In this great enterprise, which delights me

In so many ways, as it should. And yet,
My impatience is growing all the time.
He doesn't seem capable of finishing,
He constantly alters things, or creeps on slowly
Only to stop again, and dash one's hopes
When the end seemed near. The pleasure sours
When something promised is so long arriving.

PRINCESS

But I applaud the slow, modest care   270
He gives to the perfection of his scheme.
Only if the Muse smiles on him will he
Contrive to draw all the threads together,
And his soul's one desire is to achieve
The perfect whole. Tasso would never
Throw off some easy trifles, purely
To entertain us in a casual way
And insult our intelligence. I believe
We should leave him to work at his own pace.
Time is no measure of a work of art,   280
And if posterity is to benefit,
We should try to forget about ourselves.

ALFONSO

Then I propose that we collaborate,
As we have to our advantage in the past:
You must restrain me if I go too far,
And if I find you are too lenient,
I shall prove more forceful. Then perhaps
We shall suddenly see him achieve that goal
We so long for him to realise. Our own land
And all the world will then be astonished   290
At what he has accomplished, I shall receive
The credit due to me, and Tasso will be
Introduced to life. A noble man should not
Owe all his culture to one narrow circle:
His country and the world should play their part,
He should suffer both fame and hostility,
And have to know himself and others well.

Solitude will no longer soothe, and flatter,
Enemies will not spare him, friends *must* not,
And in such struggles he will use his powers   300
To feel just what he is – feel himself a man.

LEONORA

This means that you will have given Tasso
Everything, having already provided
So very much! Talent grows privately,
But character is formed by all the pressures
Of living in the world. O that he could
Develop his spirit at your instruction,
As he does his art! Then he might not shun others
With a suspicion breeding fear, and hate.

ALFONSO

Only he who knows nothing about mankind   310
Finds people frightening. The kind of man
Who shrinks from human beings will misjudge them.
Tasso is such a one, and gradually
He will lock his free spirit in confusions.
Do you know, there are times when he throws away
All dignity in worrying himself
About my favour! He will mistrust
A hundred people who are not his enemies:
Sometimes it happens that a servant leaves him,
Letters get lost, or papers go astray –   320
And he immediately thinks it is
Some deliberate plot to undermine him.

PRINCESS

Dear brother – I think we should remember
That a man cannot separate himself
From what he is. If there were a friend
Out walking with us, and he hurt his foot,
Surely it would be best to walk more slowly
And lend him a willing hand?

ALFONSO
And better still
If we could heal him, or fetch a doctor
For professional advice on a cure;   330
Then, when our friend was better, we could start
Our walk again on new paths altogether.
Still, let me say just this: I shall not assume
The role of the rigorous physician.
Already I do all I can to plant
Security and trust in Tasso's heart.
Very often I give him, quite openly,
The clearest signs of very special treatment.
If he comes and brings complaints to me,
I always see they are investigated   340
– As I did recently when he imagined
His room had been broken into. If I find
No substance in his fears, then I calmly
Show him how *I* see it; and because
One must try everything, I show great patience
– Tasso deserves it, and I know that you
Will willingly support me.
                              But now!
Having brought you to the country I myself
Must go back to town this evening. Antonio
Is coming here from Rome: you may just catch him,   350
But we have so much to talk about, and settle,
That we ought to return to Ferrara.

PRINCESS
May we go too?

ALFONSO
Do stay here in Belriguardo
– Or go over together to Consandoli.
You are free to enjoy these beautiful days
To the full, as the fancy takes you.

PRINCESS
Can't you stay with us? You could just as well
Do your talking here as in the city –

LEONORA
And you won't snatch Antonio away
When he'll have so much to tell us about Rome—?   360

ALFONSO
Please, children, children! Look, I promise you,
Antonio and I will hurry back
As quickly as we can. You shall hear his news,
And help me to reward him for the trouble
He has once again taken to serve me.
Then, when our business is settled, we'll let
The crowd in for a great celebration
— And if the company happens to include
Some beautiful woman, I might enjoy
Meeting her in some corner of this grove—   370

LEONORA
While we looked the other way?

ALFONSO
                              I would myself,
If you needed the same kind of favour!

PRINCESS
(looking offstage)
I have been watching Tasso approaching.
He's been coming towards us — so slowly —
And every so often he stands still
As if he can't decide . . . Then he starts again,
A little faster . . . Then, again, he falters —

ALFONSO
If he is writing, don't distract him! Let him
Wander where he likes.

PRINCESS
No — he's coming this way.

(Enter Tasso, carrying a volume bound in parchment.)

SCENE 3

Princess; Leonora; Alfonso; Tasso.

TASSO
I hesitated about coming here,   380
And even now I don't know that I should.
It isn't finished – I must make that plain
In case you thought it was . . . On the other hand,
I felt this sudden fear: what if I looked
Too nervous, or ungrateful for your goodness?
So – as a man can only stand and say
'Here I am!' and hope that his good friends
Will be pleased to see him – in the same spirit,
I can but offer you this book and ask
'Will you take it, please? . . . For what it is?'   390

(He hands the volume to Alfonso.)

ALFONSO
What a marvellous surprise! You have turned my day
Into a festival. So now, at last,
I can hold it in my hands – and in one sense
I can call it mine. It has seemed an age,
Waiting for you to come to me and say,
'I have finished! All my work on it is done!'

TASSO
If you are satisfied, then it is finished:
This book belongs to you in *every* sense.
When I was thinking merely of the effort
Put into making it, or saw it only   400
As all that writing scored on all those pages,
Then I could truly say, 'This work is mine.'
But when I consider it more deeply,
When I ask myself what gives it any value,
Any essential worth it might possess,
I have to say, 'I owe it to you alone.'
If Nature did fortuitously grant me
Her gift of poetry, I also knew

The ruthlessness of Fortune, capable
Of viciously thrusting me aside . . .
When I was young, all the glamours of the world   410
Enticed me, but the plight of my dear parents
Blotted such visions out – their misery
Hushed all my singing lines into laments
For their deep suffering; my poems were
My private cadences of grief, for them.
It was you who discovered me at that time,
And raised me from that life to live and grow
In a lovely freedom! You lifted all
That weight of sorrow from me, and allowed   420
My soul to expand in song. And if my work
Should win any praise at all, I would feel
That you deserved it – it belongs to you.

ALFONSO
For saying that, you deserve the higher praise
– For so modestly including us in it!

TASSO
But please, won't you understand me? I believe,
Believe profoundly, that I owe this book
To you and no one else. Could this mere youth
Have found it in himself to write this poem?
Could he have written about strategy,   430
Or skill in the handling of arms? About
The counsels of great generals, and the brilliant
Ventures of famous knights? About the vigilance
Which lies awake to intercept the secret
Cunning of subtle enemies? My lord,
I found in you alone the inspiration
To write this book: you were my guiding spirit,
Letting your unattainably high nature
Shine out through the efforts of a mortal.

PRINCESS
Can't you simply enjoy our pleasure in it –?   440

ALFONSO
Happy to know that all good men will praise it –?

LEONORA
And very proud, to know it makes you famous?

TASSO
This moment itself is all I wish for.
While I worked, all my thoughts were only
Of my dearest friends: I longed so much
To please you, if I could – if a man can't see
The whole world in his friends, he does not deserve
To be known by the world at large. My one true home
Is here, where my soul must stay and learn   450
All the lessons that experience, learning, taste
Can give me; as I look at you, I see
Standing in front of me the world itself
And all posterity! Great crowds of people
Confuse an artist; only those like you,
Who understand, should judge him and reward him.

ALFONSO
If, as you say, we represent the world
And all posterity, we cannot just
Receive and do nothing. – Over here
We have that very token of achievement   460
Which we keep for the poet; even heroes
Will not grudge it to the one they need so much.
          (He indicates the head of Virgil, crowned with
                         the laurel.)
Was it pure chance? Or did some guiding spirit
Weave this wreath for us, and leave it here?
How opportune it is to find it resting
On your ancestor's brow. I seem to hear
Great Virgil say to us, 'Why crown the dead?
They had rewards and joys enough in life,
And if you honour us, then let the living
Have their share also. I have been crowned enough,   470
And these green branches should belong to life.'

(Alfonso beckons to the Princess. She takes the wreath from Virgil's head, and goes to Tasso with it. He steps back.)

LEONORA
Why – don't you want to take it? See whose hand
Presents you with an everlasting crown!

TASSO
Let me consider, please . . . I cannot see
How I could go on living after this –

ALFONSO
The sudden thought of it may scare you now,
But you will learn to wear it happily.

PRINCESS
(she holds up the wreath)
Tasso – I feel a rare and strange delight
In telling you my thoughts without even speaking.

TASSO
I will take it on my head, then – but only   480
From your dear hands, and kneeling to receive it.

(He kneels; and the Princess places the wreath on his head.)

LEONORA
(applauding)
Long live our poet, crowned with the one wreath
Fitting his talent *and* his modesty!

(Tasso stands up.)

ALFONSO
And see this as a rehearsal for the great
Day of your crowning on the Capitol –

PRINCESS
– To the sound of applause from mightier crowds
Than this little group of your closest friends.

TASSO

Take it away again! *Take it away!*
It sears my hair like a ray from the sun
Falling too hot upon my head, and scorching   490
My thoughts away to nothing. I feel it
Like a fever, stirring in my veins.
Forgive me. It is too much for me to bear.

LEONORA

But don't you see? This wreath is your protection
Against the heat of fame: it cools the brow
Which has to suffer all the stress of genius.

TASSO

I am not worthy of such protection
– That is meant only for the heads of heroes.
Please raise it up again, you gods, to float
Transformed among the highest clouds, beyond   500
My reach once more. Then all my life I might
Perpetually struggle to achieve it.

ALFONSO

The earlier a man succeeds in life
The sooner will he learn to know the value
Of life's richest prizes. Thus he won't let them
Easily slip away – because he knows
How to arm himself to preserve them.

TASSO

And yes, whoever arms himself like that
Feels in his heart an everlasting strength.
For me, this moment, all my strength has gone.   510
This happiness has drained away the courage
That taught me to confront misfortune
Without ever flinching, and to meet injustice
With pride. Has this joy and this delight
Even dissolved the marrow in my limbs,
And left them trembling? . . . Once again I kneel

In front of you, Princess. I plead with you,
Take it away, so I might feel my life
New and fresh again inside me, as if
I were waking from a wonderful dream.　　　　　　520

PRINCESS
If you can modestly and quietly bear
The gift the gods have made you, will you not try
To wear our wreath with the same peace of mind?
This is our finest gift; and once a head
Which is worthy to receive them wears
These leaves, they will rest on that head for ever.

TASSO
Then let me leave this place in shame, and hide
My happiness deep among these trees
Where I once hid my desolation.
I'll go alone, with no eyes to remind me　　　　　530
Of my undeserved happiness. And if
I see by chance, reflected in a spring,
An image wonderfully crowned, held there
In a still stretch of the heavens between
The trees and the rocks, and resting there
In meditation, then it will seem
I am gazing on Elysium itself,
Spread out on the surface of that mirror,
As if by magic. I will ask myself,
Who is this young man, in his solitude?　　　　　540
Does he come from the past, to stand here crowned?
What is his name? What are his qualities?
I shall wait there long and silently, and think
If only someone else, and then another,
Would appear and speak to him! If I could see
All the heroes, all the poets of the past
Flocking to join him in that glass, all met
And joined inseparably, just as
They were in life itself! A magnet's force
Draws iron to iron, and the task they share　　　　550
Binds poet and hero together. Homer gave

The whole of his life to the contemplation
Of two great heroes – and Alexander,
On entering Elysium, hurries off
To seek out both Achilles *and* Homer.
If only I could be there – see their souls
United now in fellowship in heaven.

LEONORA
Come back to us! You have left us standing here
Forgotten while you dream about the past.

TASSO
I only appear to be dreaming, I am   560
Here in the present, and it overwhelms me!

PRINCESS
I am happy to hear you speak with spirits:
You speak so humanly, I love to hear it.

(A page steps up and delivers a message to the Prince.)

ALFONSO
He has arrived! – Yes, bring him here at once.
He comes at just the right time. – Here he is!

(Enter Antonio.)

SCENE 4

Princess; Leonora; Alfonso; Tasso; Antonio.

Antonio, not only do you bring
Yourself, you bring your good news also!

PRINCESS
                                        Welcome back!

ANTONIO
I hardly dare confess how pleased I am
To be back with you again; your company
Guarantees all the pleasures I have missed   570
For a very long time. Besides, your kind
Approval of what I achieved in Rome
Is a splendid reward for all those days
Dragged out impatiently, or even wasted
On the mere hope of advantage. But at last
We have what we want, our struggle is over.

LEONORA
Antonio, it's wonderful to see you,
But you choose to come just as I have to leave.

ANTONIO
Well – something always ruins my good luck!
Much of my pleasure will vanish with you.   580

TASSO
I welcome you, as well. I hope to enjoy
The company of one with such experience.

ANTONIO
If ever you could look out from your world
Into mine, you would find I could be trusted.

ALFONSO
Antonio! – in your letters you've already
Told me what you have done, and how things went;
But I still have a great deal to ask you
Concerning how you brought all this about.
If you want success in Rome, you need to judge
Each move precisely, and the man who slaves   590
Too earnestly to serve his lord's advantage
Meets little sympathy: Rome will snatch all
He offers, and in turn pay little back.
If a man goes to Rome with too much hope
Of winning something, he may leave with nothing,
And even if he goes in a giving mood,
He will be lucky with the smallest gains.

ANTONIO

Nothing I did – no skill that I could show –
Would account for our success: the most
Adroit of diplomats would surely meet   600
His master in the Vatican. No, I found
That a series of happy chances helped me
In the planning of my tactics. Gregory
– The worthiest ever to wear his crown –
Greets you and honours you, sends his blessing
And speaks with joy of the day he embraced you.
As a discerning judge of men he knows
That you merit all his praise and his support.

ALFONSO

Praise from Pope Gregory, when it is sincere
Is flattering. But looking down from Rome,   610
A Pope sees kingdoms at his feet, their princes
Shrunk to the size of puppets. Antonio,
We will not delude ourselves. I want to know
What really helped you in the Vatican.

ANTONIO

Well, if you really want to know, it was
The Pope's own supreme good sense.
To him, the small looks small, the great seems great.
In order to control the world he'll gladly
Make graceful concessions to his neighbours,
And if he ceded you that strip of land,
He did it for something better – your goodwill.   620
He wants to see his Italy at peace,
With friends ranged all around him; then the power
Of the Christendom he rules can turn to face
The Turks and the heretics, and destroy them.

PRINCESS

Do we know who are the men he favours most?
Which ones are his closest advisors?

ANTONIO

Men of experience and energy
– No one else wins his confidence or favour.
Having served the cause of Rome from early youth,   630
He governs it now, controlling all those courts
Where he spent long years as an ambassador,
And guided them even then. He sees the world
As clearly as he sees the advantage
Of his own Roman state; and just to watch
This Pope in action is to marvel at
The way time brings to fullness all those schemes
He was planting so quietly in the past.
The world can offer us no finer sight
Than a clever prince in charge of a realm   640
Where each of his subjects believes he serves himself
In his proud obedience, because his tasks
Are only what a just lord asks of him.

LEONORA

I should love some time to observe at close quarters
A nation like that.

ALFONSO

Oh yes, I know! I'm sure
You would love to meddle in it too; Leonora
Could never stand by and look on. And besides,
It might be very pleasant to join hands
With women in these high counsels – might it not!

LEONORA
(to Alfonso)
You are not going to tease me, I promise you –!   650

ALFONSO
But I owe you some teasing from the past –

LEONORA
If I am still in credit with you, then
Allow me to go on – stop interrupting!

(to Antonio)

Does the Pope reward all his close friends?

ANTONIO

No more nor less than is justified. A prince
Who never helped his friends would earn reproach
From the common people even. Gregory
Knows how to make use of the best talent,
And since his friends all serve him loyally,
He fulfils two sorts of obligation: 660
To his country *and* his friends.

TASSO

What does he do for learning and the arts?
Does he promote them? – Seek in that way
To emulate great princes of the past?

ANTONIO

Gregory honours learning where it helps
In teaching how to govern his great city
And understand other nations. He values art
So far as it adds to the glory of his Rome,
Helping to make its palaces and churches
The wonder of the world. Or, to be blunt,   670
These things have to serve a useful purpose.

ALFONSO

Yes . . . But Antonio, how long will it take
To tie up the loose ends? Do you foresee
Any obstacles put up to hinder us?

ANTONIO

No, I think not. I should be quite surprised
If we couldn't settle everything fairly soon,
With your signature to one or two letters.

ALFONSO

Then my whole life is pleasure and advantage!
My boundaries are extended, and made safe

For the years ahead – and you managed that 680
Without one violent action. You deserve
Some high civic honour; one day, I know,
These ladies will weave you a crown of oak-leaves
And place it on your head. And meanwhile, Tasso
Has enriched me in other ways: in his book,
Jerusalem is delivered,
And our modern Christendom put to shame.
He set himself the very highest goal,
But his marvellous courage and application
Have seen him to the end. He stands here wearing 690
The finest crown of all, for his great labours.

ANTONIO
So the mystery is solved! And I know now
Why *two* crowned heads were here to welcome me.

TASSO
You can see my joy before your eyes . . .
If only you could see, in the same glance,
All the deep confusion of my spirit.

ANTONIO
This is the effect of Alfonso's lavish
Generosity – you are just discovering
What any of his subjects knows about.

PRINCESS
When you have seen what Tasso has achieved, 700
You will discover that we are being
Very moderate with our rewards: they are
The earliest, faintest whispers of a praise
Posterity will echo ten times over.

ANTONIO
Isn't it fame already, to succeed
With company like this? With you for critics,
Who would question the accolades? – But tell me, please,
Who made this wreath for Ariosto?

LEONORA

I did.

ANTONIO

And that was excellent! A wreath of flowers
Suits him far better than plain laurel would.   710
As Nature drapes her cloak of richest green
On the fertile earth, so Ariosto
Dresses in lustrous fable everything
That makes mankind worth honouring, and loving.
All of men's finest attributes are there,
Enshrined in his poems: intellect, good taste,
Experience, contentment, understanding,
Pure feeling for what is good – all of these things
Are there in spirit, or even (one might say)
'Bodied forth' as living persons, under trees   720
Which lightly cover them with snowy blossoms
– Or garlanded with roses while gentle cupids
Hover in careless play over their heads.
Nearby the spring of plenty gushes out,
Teeming with brilliant fishes, while above,
Rare birds fill all the air, and field and wood
Throng with huge herds of strange and splendid beasts.
In this green thicket Mischief lurks and hides,
From that high golden cloud old Wisdom utters
Sage and exalted truths, and on his lute,   730
At pure, wild random, Madness meanwhile plays
Weird notes that all-miraculously blend
In faultless harmonies! – Whoever dares
To be compared with one like Ariosto
Deserves his wreath – for sheer audacity.
Oh – please forgive me! I forgot myself,
And where I was – even what I was saying.
All these wreaths and poets, and the festive clothes
Of our young ladies, carried me away   740
Into lands of dream and inspiration.

PRINCESS
You so much prize the talent of the one
That you shall not underestimate the other.
One day you shall interpret Tasso for us:
We praise, but you will help us understand.

ALFONSO
Well now, Antonio – there are several things
I am curious to know. When we are done,
The ladies may have you to themselves
For the rest of the day! – Will you let us go?

(Exit Antonio with Alfonso; Tasso follows the ladies.)

ACT TWO

A room.

SCENE 1

Princess; Tasso.

TASSO

Princess – am I allowed to follow you?   750
My soul is plagued with thoughts which will not settle
Into proper sense, or order. Solitude
Lures me back constantly by whispering
'Come, and I'll clear away all these new doubts
Which so disturb your heart.' But if I see you,
If my listening ear should catch one single
Word from your lips, all my fetters fall away
And a new day is born around me!
I will confess to you: the man who joined us   760
Unexpectedly just now, did not
Give me a very kind awakening
From my lovely dream. His character
– The very words he spoke – affected me
So strangely, that I feel myself far more
Divided than I ever was, still more
Weighed down by all my conflicts and confusions.

PRINCESS

When an old friend has lived away from us
For a long stretch of time, and grown accustomed
To an unusual life, should we expect
To see no change in him when he comes back?   770
Antonio is no different in himself:
When we have lived with him a few more days,
The strings will gradually be tuned again,
And all the present discords be resolved

In one perfect harmony. By that time,
He should have gained a better understanding
Of what you have achieved; then he will see
That you rank as highly as that poet
He sets up as a giant beside you.

TASSO
But my Princess! – his praise of Ariosto   780
Delighted me. What reason would I have
To be offended? Are we not reassured
When someone speaks in praise of the man
Who stands as our great exemplar? In our hearts,
We can silently say this: If you could show
Some trace of his high talent, then some part
Of his fame might come with it! Oh no,
What moved me most profoundly – and even now
It fills my soul completely – were the figures
Of that huge, seething, restless world which moves   790
In its majestic progress round one great
Supremely clever man, fulfilling
The whole course which this demigod has ventured
To mark out as its destiny. I listened
Eagerly to Antonio, because
He speaks from such experience! But oh,
The more I heard, the more my self-esteem
Drained away: I feared that I might vanish
Like Echo among the rocks, losing myself
Like a reverberation, a mere nothing.   800

PRINCESS
But just before, you seemed to feel so clearly
That the poet and the hero lived their lives
For one another, seeking each other out
With no need for jealousy. The deed
Which is worthy of a verse is splendid;
But to hand down such deeds in poetry
To all posterity – that is splendid too!
Why not just watch the wild course of the world
From this quiet river bank? Let our peaceful
Land be your haven and protection?   810

TASSO

Was it not in this land that I first saw
How gloriously the brave are rewarded,
And marvelled at the sight! I first came here
As an inexperienced youth, in those great days
When festival on festival made Ferrara
The seat of chivalry. What a sight that was!
Round the arena where high skill and courage
Paraded in their splendour, sat a throng
Of lovely women and distinguished men,
And the sun will not shine on their like again.   820
And gazing on their beauty and distinction,
One cried aloud, in sheer astonishment,
'This Italy, this narrow land the ocean
Almost encircles, she has sent them here;
Together they make the most glorious court
That ever sat in judgement upon honour,
Merit or virtue. Go through them all,
Number them one by one, you will not find
One single man or woman sitting there
Who needs to feel ashamed beside his neighbour!   830
Then the lists were opened, and the beat of hooves
Thundered upon our ears; light, everywhere,
Glinted on shields and helmets as the knights
Rode out to the scream of fanfares; and as lance
Thrust against lance and shattered, helmets and shields
Rang loud with the sound! The swirling dust
Covered the victor's pride, and hid away
The miserable shame of the defeated
– Oh let *me* hide that whole bright spectacle
From my vivid memory! On this happy day   840
It makes me feel my own unworthiness.

PRINCESS

If all that noble circle and those deeds
Inspired you at that time, spurring you on
To effort and endeavour, I myself
Could still have helped to show you something else:
The lesson of patience. I did not see

Those famous festivals you praise so much,
And which a hundred tongues all praised to me
Then, and for many years. All of that time
I lay enclosed in pain, and suffering,   850
And sick despair – shut in a silence
Where the last echo of that joy died out
With scarcely an interruption. Death's image
Hovered in front of me on outspread wings,
Blocking out any view of all this various
And ever-changing world . . . Then gradually,
It drew away. And I saw, as through a veil,
The lovely colours of this life again,
Faint, but still pleasant; and figures stirring . . .
And the first time I stepped outside my sickroom,   860
Supported by my ladies, Lucretia came
(So radiantly alive!) and she brought you,
Leading you by the hand, new and unknown,
The first to meet me as I came to life.
I had such hopes that day, for both of us,
And so far they have never been betrayed.

TASSO
I was bewildered by the swarming crowds;
The sight of so much splendour blinded me,
And stirred by what I'd seen, I went in silence   870
Down quiet passages at your sister's side
To step into that room where you came forward
On the arms of your ladies – that moment
Is unforgettable! Forgive me! As a man
Possessed by evil spirits can, quite freely,
Quite easily be cured of all his madness
By the presence of a god, so was I, also,
Cured of my every fantasy and passion,
And healed of all false motives I might have had
When my gaze met your gaze. Before that time   880
My callow longing had gone chasing out
After a thousand dreams and vanities.
Now I drew back inside myself, and felt
Ashamed; because I now at last could tell

What was worth the seeking. – And to think I might
Have tried to plunder all the sea's wide shores
For the pearl hidden in one silent shell!

PRINCESS
That was the first of many happy days,
And if the young Duke of Urbino had not
Taken my sister from us, *all* our days   890
Would have passed in calm delight. But alas,
We have to live without her carefree spirit,
Her heart so full of courage and life,
All the wit and charm of that fine lady.

TASSO
I know that all too well: ever since the day
Lucretia left us, there has hardly been
One who could bring such pure joy back to you.
Your loss has given such deep grief to me!
Often I wander through that grove in anguish,
Crying out to myself, 'Must it be only   900
Her sister who can claim the happiness,
The right, to be so much to this dear lady?
Is there no other worthy heart she might
Entrust herself to? No longer any spirit
Who would be in tune with her? Have mind
And wit become extinct? And this one woman,
However admirable she might be,
Was she everything?' Princess, forgive me,
Many a time I thought about myself –
Could I be something to you, even
In the smallest way? And not with words, but deeds?   910
Then my actions would show you just how much
My heart was yours in secret. But I failed,
Time after time I blundered and upset you,
Offended someone whom you were protecting,
Muddled some question which you wanted clear
– And when I most yearned to draw close to you,
I felt myself slipping away.

PRINCESS

I have never misunderstood you, Tasso.
I also know how active you can be
In doing yourself harm. My sister   920
Knew how to make friends with anyone,
Whoever they were; but you have not made
One friend here in all these years.

TASSO

                 It is my fault!
But tell me, where is the man or woman
In all the world whom I would dare open
My heart to – as I open it to you?

PRINCESS

You ought to put more trust in my brother.

TASSO

But your brother is my Prince! You must not think
The wild desire for freedom governs me!
Man is not born to be free; and there is not   930
A greater happiness for a noble man
Than to serve a prince whom he respects.
No, he is my lord, and I am thoroughly
Sensible of the meaning of that word:
I must learn to be silent when he speaks,
I must do as he commands, even if
My heart and my mind rebel against it.

PRINCESS

That can never be so with my brother!
Besides, now that Antonio is back,
You have a new friend rich in worldly wisdom.   940

TASSO

I hoped so once, but now I despair of it.
There might be much to learn from knowing him,
His advice might be extremely useful,
I could well say that he possesses

All the things I lack – but when the gods
Crowded with gifts around Antonio's cradle,
Unfortunately the Graces were not there,
And whoever lacks the blessings of those fair ones
May well possess much, and have much to give
– But he takes no one into his heart.   950

PRINCESS

But you may confide in him, and that
Is very important. You must not ask for
Everything from just one man. Antonio
Will carry out his promises, and once
He declares himself your friend, he will provide
Whatever you lack. I must see you two
Joined together as friends! I flatter myself
I can do it – if you do not oppose me
As you usually do. And Leonora,
Who has been here a long time: she is refined,   960
And elegant, and easy to get on with.
You have not been so close as *she* would like.

TASSO

I have always listened carefully to you
When you speak of Leonora – otherwise
I would have withdrawn from her altogether.
Although she can appear to be so kind,
I can rarely be very open with her:
When she sets about trying to help her friends,
It is so very clear that she is *trying*.

PRINCESS

Tasso, do you honestly think that this   970
Is the way to make friends? This path leads us astray
Into solitary woods and silent valleys.
More and more you indulge your feelings, and strive
To set up inside your imagination
A Golden Age which the real world cannot
Provide for you – the harder you search
The less are you likely to find it.

TASSO

Princess, do you know what you are saying?
Once long ago there was a Golden Age,
But where has it flown to? All hearts long in vain   980
For the time when men roamed freely on this earth
Like happy herds, all innocent in pleasure;
When, in each shining field, an ancient tree
Gave shade to a shepherd and a shepherdess,
And the fresh woods spread close and tender branches
Round passionate young love; when, clear and still,
On beds of purest sand, the gentle stream
Softly embraced the nymphs; when the frightened snake
Fled harmlessly to safety through the grass,
And the young huntsman roused and chased away   990
The daring faun; when all the birds that flew
In the freedom of the air, and every beast
Grazing the hills and valleys cried to men,
'You may do whatever brings delight.'

PRINCESS

My friend, that Golden Age is long since past
– Though the good may have power to bring it back.
But shall I now admit what *I* believe?
The Golden Age the poet woos us with
– That lovely age – existed no more then
Than it does today; although I would allow   1000
That if a kind of world resembling it
Existed, it is certainly a world
We may regain, whenever kindred spirits
Gather to share the pleasures of this earth.
But will you change just one word of your maxim?
– 'You may do whatever things are *right*.'

TASSO

Oh if there could be one universal
Court of the very best and wisest men
To determine what was 'right'! Each man
Imagines that what suits him best is right,   1010
And all the time, clever and powerful men
Get the best of things – and do just what they like.

PRINCESS
If you wish to know exactly what is right,
You need only speak to noble women.
They most of all are anxious that everything
Should be right, and seemly. Our sex is gentle,
A high wall of propriety stands round it
For its own safety. Where propriety reigns,
Women's voices will prevail; where only
Baseness is found, in that place they are nothing.   1020
If you asked about the sexes, I would say this:
Men strive for freedom, women for rules of conduct.

TASSO
Then are all men coarse and insensitive?

PRINCESS
No, not at all. But you aim at distant goals,
And your striving must be violent. You dare
To act for all eternity, while women
Limit themselves to something finite,
And want to preserve *that* for ever.
No woman can be sure of a man's heart,   1030
Not even if he promised it to her once
Most ardently: beauty is transient,
And beauty is the only thing that men
Seem to honour in a woman; what remains
When beauty fades away has no attractions,
And might as well be dead. If only
There were men in this world who really knew
How to treasure a woman's heart – they would find
Such a wealth of constancy and love contained
In a woman's being. If the memory
Of single hours of loveliness stayed alive,   1040
If your fine perception could also pierce
The veil which old age or sickness finally
Casts over every one of us, and if
Possession, which should bring you peace of mind,
Did not make you still more covetous, we might
See the dawning of a splendid day indeed,
And celebrate our own Golden Age.

TASSO
While you were speaking there came back to me
Certain fears I had almost forgotten . . .

PRINCESS
Tasso, what do you mean? Be frank with me.   1050

TASSO
I have already heard it, oh so often,
And recently I have heard it again
– If I hadn't heard it, I would certainly
Have thought it myself . . . Noble princes
Are suing for your hand. We may fear things
We know are likely . . . and simply despair.
You will leave us – and how can we bear it!

PRINCESS
Don't be anxious about it for the moment.
I might even say: Don't let it worry you
At any time. You know I love this place   1060
And want to stay here; I know of nothing
That would lure me away. But if you want
To keep me, live in harmony with us:
Your happiness would make *me* happier.

TASSO
Teach me the possibility of that!
My days are given to you, and when my heart
Opens to praise and thank you, only then
Do I know the highest joy, a strange, divine
Pleasure that you alone can give. This way   1070
Are the gods among us marked out from others,
As the highest destiny stands out above
The counsel and the will of even
The cleverest of men. Where we see mighty
Wave after wave break round us, they stand firm,
Letting them lap their feet like gentle ripples,
Not noticing the furious storm which beats
At our heads and hurls us down; they do not hear
Our pleas for help, they let us fill the air

With sighs and lamentations as if they were   1080
The cries of fretful children, capable
Of nothing more. O Princess, goddess,
You have been so patient with me; like the sun,
Your glance has dried the dew of all my tears.

PRINCESS

It is wholly right that women should treat you
In the friendliest way: in many ways your poem
Exalts our sex, and you have always known
How to make your women lovable and noble,
Be they gentle or courageous. And although
Armida may seem hateful, even in her   1090
There is some charm and beauty to redeem her.

TASSO

Whatever lives and vibrates in my poem
I owe to one person, one alone.
But this is no vague image shining out
Before my mind and dazzling my soul
Only to fade and vanish. My own eyes
Have seen the archetype of every virtue,
And every beauty. All that I made,
And fashioned in that mould, that will endure!
– Tancred's heroic passion for Clorinda,   1100
Erminia's unseen faithfulness, maintained
So long in silence, fair Sophronia's
Greatness of heart, and pure Olinda's pain –
None of these are mere shades or fantasies,
I know they are eternal – they are real!
What has more right to last for centuries
And go on moving people, than the secret
Of a noble love set down in graceful song?

PRINCESS

And shall I tell you of another merit
That has crept unnoticed into this poem?   1110
It gradually entices us to listen,
And then – as we listen – we understand,

And when we understand it, we just cannot
Find fault with what it says – we are won over!

TASSO

Princess, you open up all heaven for me;
And if my eyes can bear to watch this splendour,
I shall see my own eternal happiness
Descending on rays of golden light!

PRINCESS

But Tasso, listen please. In this life
There are things we should seize upon with passion,   1120
And others we can only hope to win
Through moderation and self-sacrifice.
Among these there is virtue – and there is love,
Which is linked with it. Think deeply about that!

(Exit.)

SCENE 2

TASSO
(alone)

Can you open your eyes and look around you?
You are alone . . . Did these pillars hear
What she was saying? Do you need to fear
These witnesses of your great happiness?
The sun has risen now on a new age   1130
Unlike any other I have known!
In an instant the goddess has descended
And lifted the mortal up. I find a land
I have never seen before, an entire new world
Where my deepest and most ardent wish
Is most richly granted. Once I used to dream
I was close to the greatest happiness,
But now I know a world of happiness
More real than any dreaming! A man born blind

Imagines lights and colours as best he can,
But then if daylight suddenly breaks in
And banishes his blindness, that is no less
Than a new sense for him. And that is what   1140
You give to me – a path that stretches out
Into the distance, and I follow it
With courage, and wild hope, and drunken joy.
You give so much, you give me glorious gifts,
And the way you rain them down is the way
Earth and heaven themselves bestow them,
Their hands full and lavish in the giving.
And in return you only ask the things
Such gifts entitle you to ask: I must
Achieve self-sacrifice, be moderate
So that I might deserve your confidence.
What have I ever done that she should choose me?
What must I do to be worthy of her now?   1150
She confided in you – thus you are worthy.
Yes, princess, let me dedicate my soul
To your words and your glances for ever:
Demand whatever you want, I am yours.
If she sends me away to foreign lands,
Looking for danger, sacrifice or fame,
Or hands the golden lyre to me, that I
Might sing her praises here, in the quiet grove,
I am equally hers, to make of what she will.
She possesses all my being, every treasure   1160
I store in my heart shall be hers. If a god
Had given me a thousand times my talent,
I could not start to utter what I feel,
Or find words for my adoration.
I would need the painter's hand, the poet's tongue
Sweet with the earliest honey of the year.
No, Tasso shall no longer lose himself
And be lonely – weak – cast down, among the trees
And all mankind. Tasso is not alone,
He is with you. Let me see the noblest deeds,   1170
Surrounded with dreadful dangers! – I would go on
And gladly risk the life I gain from her.

I would summon the best of men as my friends
To do the impossible, a noble band
Which would act at her bidding. O rash man,
Why did you not stay silent, wait your time
To fall at her feet as worthy of her,
And worthier still? That was what you planned,   1180
Your clever wish. But let it be this way!
To have this pure and undeserved reward
Is pleasanter than imagining you had
Some kind of claim to it. Look joyful now!
What lies ahead of you is vast, is boundless!
A youthful hope returns, and lures you on
To an unknown, shining future. So, take heart!
O Fortune, favour this sapling just this once!   1190
It strives towards heaven, it lifts a thousand boughs
– And each one blossoms! Let it bear golden fruit,
Let it bear joy, and let her dear hand pluck
The treasure from its branches!

(Enter Antonio.)

SCENE 3

Tasso; Antonio.

Welcome, sir!
I see you now as if for the first time!
Was ever man commended to me so highly!
I know you now, and value your true worth.
I want to offer you my heart and hand
Without the slightest reservation.   1200
I hope you are not thinking to reject me?

ANTONIO
These are handsome gifts. And yes, you offer them
Most generously. I see their value.
So will you kindly let me hesitate
Before accepting them? I am not yet sure

I can offer the same things in return.
I would not wish to seem precipitate
– Or ungrateful. Let me be prudent for us both.

TASSO

Yes . . . Who would blame you. Almost any step
One takes in life reveals how necessary   1210
Prudence can be. But then, how wonderful
When instinct says you need not be so cautious.

ANTONIO

Each man must decide that for himself:
He is the one who pays for his own mistakes.

TASSO

I see . . . Well then, my duty is performed.
I have honoured her wishes to the letter.
She wanted us to be friends, and so I came
To present myself to you. Antonio,
I dared not hold back, and yet I would not
Want to press the matter. In time perhaps   1220
It may seem easier for you to claim
The gift you refuse with such cold contempt.

ANTONIO

A moderate man is often thought cold by those
Who, when a sudden heat takes charge of them,
Assume they are warmer than other people.

TASSO

I condemn such failings, just as you do:
I may be young, but I know that I prefer
A constant man to an impetuous one.

ANTONIO

That's wise of you! See you don't change your mind.

TASSO

You are quite entitled to advise me,   1230
Even to warn me, seeing that you have

Experience to guide you as a friend.
But please believe me: a quiet heart
Will heed the warnings of each day and hour,
And practise secretly the very virtues
You think to teach me for the first time now.

ANTONIO
It would be pleasant to be so absorbed
With one's own self – if only it served a purpose.
But no man ever comes to true self-knowledge
Through introspection. He will rate himself   1240
Too humbly – or too highly, sad to say!
Self-knowledge comes through knowing other people:
Only life can teach a man what he really is.

TASSO
I respect what you say, and I agree.

ANTONIO
And yet you are thinking something quite different
From all I have been trying to tell you.

TASSO
None of this brings us closer to each other.
It is not clever, and it does no good,
To mistake a man on purpose, no matter
Who he might be. It hardly needed   1250
The word of the Princess: from the very start
I recognised you easily, as one
Who sets out to do good, and who succeeds.
You don't aim to serve yourself, you serve
Other people; and your heart stays constant,
However much the tides of life may vary.
That is how I see you. So how could I
Not want to make a friend of you, and share
In that vast treasure of fine qualities
Which you keep locked inside you? Let me swear it:
You would have no reason to be sorry if   1260
You opened your heart. Knowing me better,

You would be my friend. – I have so long needed
A friend like you. I am inexperienced
And young, but not ashamed of that. The future
Still glows like a golden cloud round my head.
O noble man, will you take me to your heart?
Teach me self-sacrifice, and moderation?

ANTONIO

So: in one single moment you hope to gain
What time alone, and the very greatest care –   1270

TASSO

But in one single moment love can grant
Far more than might be gained in endless years!
Please realise – I don't ask this – I demand it!
I dare to demand it in the name of virtue,
Which always unites good men. And now
Shall I mention another name? The Princess
Hopes it will happen, the Princess Leonora
Longs to unite us two in friendship!
Shouldn't we grant her wish, shouldn't we go
As one man, now, to the goddess, offering   1280
Our service to her, offering our whole souls
To do the best we can for her together?
Here is my hand again – take hold of it,
Don't shrink back and refuse. O noble man,
Give me that pleasure which all good men know
– The joy of yielding unreservedly
To one so much better than themselves.

ANTONIO

The wind is in your sails; it seems as if
You have won your success too easily.
You expect to find broad highways, and gates   1290
Wide open to you everywhere. I wish you
All honour and fortune, but I know too well
That the gulf between us is too great.

TASSO
There is a gap – in years and in achievement –
But in courage and will-power I yield to none.

ANTONIO
But will-power alone will not provide you
With guaranteed success; and courage may
Convince you that effort does not matter.
He who achieves his aim will win the crown
– While he who is worthy often goes without;   1300
Though obviously there are many paltry wreaths
You can win by just sauntering along.

TASSO
And there are certain gifts a god will grant
Freely to one man, while denying them
To others, however much they crave them!

ANTONIO
If Fortune is that god, I would agree:
In all cases Fortune chooses blind.

TASSO
Justice also wears a blindfold
And closes her eyes to all deception.

ANTONIO
He who is lucky always praises Fortune.   1310
If she once smiles on him, he credits her
With a hundred eyes, superb intelligence,
And powerful judgement. Call her Minerva,
Call her what he likes, he wears her offerings
As if the gifts of chance were hard-earned honours.

TASSO
You make yourself very clear. What you say
Allows me to see right inside your heart
And know you for ever. Oh if only
My Princess knew you this way! Don't waste

Those arrows in your eyes and in your tongue: 1320
You aim in vain at the laurels on my head,
Which will never fade. If you could summon up
Sufficient greatness not to envy me,
You might perhaps allow yourself some right
To question my possession of this most
Supreme and sacred prize. If you could find,
If you could ever face me with, the man
Who achieves what I strive for, if you brought me
Heroes I only know from history
– Or if you found a poet to compare
With Homer, say, or Virgil, some great man   1330
Who deserved this gift three times as much as me
And was three times humbler than myself
In accepting it – then you would see me kneel
To the goddess who gave me my talents,
And not stand up until she had transferred
This crown from my head to his!

ANTONIO
Until which time you do deserve to wear it.

TASSO
I would not fear the judgement of any man
Who weighed my merits fairly; but I do not   1340
Deserve to be despised. With her own hands
My Princess made this crown, and my own Prince
Considered me worthy to receive it.

ANTONIO
Your arrogance and temper don't impress me,
And nor are they right in such a place.

TASSO
May I not do here what is right for you?
Is all truth to be banished from this palace?
Is free thought to be imprisoned here?
Must a noble man suffer oppression,
Or is not this where nobility of soul   1350

Finds its rightful place, and rejoices
In the company of great ones? Yes, it does
And shall! When our ancestors can show
A noble lineage, then we may move with princes,
And so should it be with talent: Nature
Does not grant great talent to all men,
Any more than she gives all men noble blood.
Only the meanest spirit ought to feel
Uneasy here – or an envious spirit,
Doing its shameful work as spiders would,   1360
Spinning their webs to soil these marble walls.

ANTONIO
You yourself prove that I am right to scorn you!
That a rash boy should try to force a man
Into trust and friendship! Ill-bred as you are,
What worth do you imagine you possess?

TASSO
I had rather seem ill-bred, as you describe it,
Than behave as ignobly as you.

ANTONIO
Though, of course, with a little training you might learn
Some notion of how to behave. You are young –

TASSO
But not so young as to debase myself   1370
In front of idols! I can treat scorn with scorn –

ANTONIO
If voice and verses were the only weapons,
You would be conqueror and hero too!

TASSO
It may be rash to boast about my strength
When I have never fought – but I *would* fight!

ANTONIO
And trust in the indulgence which has only
Spoiled you in all your impudence so far?

TASSO
Now, in this instant, I am become a man!
You were the last I ever would have dreamt
Of crossing swords with in the game of chance,   1380
But you heap fire on fire, and my heart
Seethes with a terrible longing for vengeance
Which will not be refused! Do you dare
To face me as the man you boast you are?

ANTONIO
You forget who *you* are, and where we stand.

TASSO
There is no sanctuary on earth compelling
A man to suffer insult and be silent.
You profane this place with your blasphemy:
I brought you the finest of all offerings,
My trust in you, respect for you – and love!
Your spirit now defiles this paradise,   1390
Your words pollute this room – not my pure heart,
Which rages against the smallest slander.

ANTONIO
This shows great spirit – for so small a body.

TASSO
It has room enough to set the spirit free.

ANTONIO
The rabble thinks abuse is showing spirit.

TASSO
Then show you are a nobleman – as I am.

ANTONIO
I show that by knowing what ground we stand on.

TASSO
Come down, then, to where we may use weapons.

ANTONIO
You should not challenge – I shall not respond.   1400

TASSO
Except with the excuses of the coward?

ANTONIO
A coward can always threaten where he is safe.

TASSO
Then I gladly sacrifice all safety!

ANTONIO
You only degrade yourself – the place you cannot.

TASSO
Then may it forgive me for my patience!

(He draws his sword.)

Either draw or follow me, or else I shall
Despise you for ever as I hate you now.

(Enter Alfonso.)

SCENE 4

Tasso; Antonio; Alfonso.

ALFONSO
In God's name! – do I find you quarrelling?

ANTONIO

Not so, my lord! You find me standing calm
In front of someone in the grip of rage.   1410

TASSO

O Prince, you are like a god come down to banish
All my anger with one glance of warning.

ALFONSO

I am astonished! – Antonio – Tasso –
How did a quarrel start here – in my house?
I thought I could regard you both as sane
Intelligent men: how could you stray so far
From the laws of civilised behaviour?

TASSO

Can you really assume you know us both?
This man may be renowned for cleverness
And honourable conduct; but he behaved
As coarsely and maliciously to me   1420
As if he were one of the rabble. When
I gave him my trust, he thrust me away;
I persevered with love, and tried again,
But he turned on me and goaded me until
All my blood had changed into bitter gall.
Forgive me: you must see I was driven mad.
If I am guilty this man is to blame!
He fed the flames of anger with a violence
Which seized on me – and injured both of us.   1430

ANTONIO

Poetic frenzy carried him away!
– My lord, I think you asked me to speak first?
If this impetuous speech-maker has finished,
May I give you my own account?

TASSO

                              Yes, do!
Go on, and tell him – tell him every word.

Each syllable shall go before this judge,
Each expression of the face. Yes, dare
To tell the truth of it, disgrace yourself
A second time – witness against yourself –
I won't disown one breath, one single pulse-beat!   1440

ANTONIO
If you wish to say more, do continue.
If not, let me speak without interruption.
My lord, would you consider it more likely
That I, or this hothead, would start a quarrel?
Which one was in the wrong? If we decide,
In the first place, to leave that matter open –

TASSO
Why leave it open? The matter of right and wrong
Is the one we should settle first of all.

ANTONIO
Taking a rather simple view of things,
One might agree –

ALFONSO
Antonio!

ANTONIO
                                My lord,   1450
I respect your hint, but can you keep him quiet!
When I have finished he may speak again,
Provided you agree. I say only this:
I cannot argue with him, neither can I
Accuse him, or even defend myself
– Nor can I give him his satisfaction.
As things now stand he forfeits his freedom,
And is subject to a rigorous law which you
May only moderate. Here, in your house,
He took it on himself to threaten me   1460
And issue challenges. He stood in front of you
Unable to conceal his naked sword.

If you had not intervened, I might
Be as guilty as he is, and disgraced.

ALFONSO
(to Tasso)
You have not done well.

TASSO
                    But my own heart
Acquits me of any guilt; and surely yours
Must absolve me also? What he says is true,
I threatened him and, yes, I drew my sword
And challenged him. But if you could have heard
The taunts he used – the calculated spite!
Every word he uttered was like a sting   1470
Infecting my blood with a new fever;
And all the time he stood there, calmly, coldly,
Holding me at a distance, cleverly
Heating up my fury, goading me
To the limits of what I could endure.
You cannot, cannot know him – I offered
The warmest, the most trusting kind of friendship,
And he threw my gift down at my feet.
If my soul had not flamed up in anger,
It would never be worthy of your favour
Or your service. If I forgot the law   1480
And where we were – forgive me! In *no* place
Will I accept contempt and suffer insult.
Wherever this heart fails you – or itself –
You must punish me, and cast me out for ever.

ANTONIO
This young man bears his heavy burdens lightly,
And brushes off grave faults like specks of dust.
It would be wonderful – if this magic art,
This poetry, wasn't famous for its trick   1490
Of playing games with the impossible.
But whether you, my lord, or this great court
Will wish to see it as a trivial matter,

I very much doubt. Majesty will extend
Protection over all who treat it as
A deity, and shelter under it.
As at an altar, every human passion
Is kept under control inside that house.
No sword shines there, no threatening word is spoken,   1500
And those insulted may not seek revenge.
The outside world is space enough for anger
And implacable temper: there no coward
Will issue threats, and no brave man turn tail.
This is a house whose walls were built securely
By your great ancestors, a solemn shrine
Fortified to proclaim their dignity.
Wisely they sealed its peace with heavy sanctions:
The guilty faced imprisonment or exile
Or even death, and there was no respect   1510
For persons, no fond clemency to weaken
The arm of justice; criminals went in fear.
Now, after this long peace, are we to see
Raw anger break all civilisation down?
My lord, you must decide and you must punish.
Who can exist within the narrow bounds
Of duty if he finds that the law itself,
And the power of his prince, will not protect him?

ALFONSO

My instincts tell me, quite impartially,
What the truth is – and I trust them more   1520
Than either of you. Would it not have been
Far better if you both had understood
Your duty, and not forced me to give judgement?
I sense that right and wrong were closely linked
In this affair. If Antonio gave offence,
Then he must find some way of giving you
Your satisfaction, though I should prefer
That you chose me to arbitrate between you.
Meanwhile, your crime makes you a prisoner, Tasso.
As I forgive you, I shall bend the law   1530
This far, for you alone: leave us, your room
Shall be the prison, and yourself the guard.

TASSO
O Prince, is this your sentence, as a judge?

ANTONIO
It is more like his mercy as a father.

TASSO
(to Antonio)
I have no more to say to you – for now.
(to Alfonso)
O Prince, if this your solemn judgement makes
A prisoner of me, then I must submit.
You have decided – I respect your word –
And I must now command my inmost heart
To be silent to its depths. But this is new . . .   1540
So new . . . I hardly know myself, or you,
Or this lovely place. Yet I know this man!
There are so many things I could reveal,
And ought to – but I will silently obey.
A crime . . . You see me as a criminal,
Or so it seems. Whatever my heart says,
The word I heard you speak was – prisoner.

ALFONSO
You take this more seriously than I do.

TASSO
I cannot grasp it yet – although perhaps
I do begin to, I am not a child.   1550
One moment all is clear, then suddenly
It clouds into confusion. Yes, I hear
My sentence, and submit . . . But even that
Is too many useless words! Weakest of men,
You must learn from now on to obey.
You forgot where you were, you dared to think
You stood among the gods, and now you find
You are cast down to destruction. So, obey.   1560
A man must willingly do some painful things.
Take first this sword, the one you gave to me

When I followed the cardinal to France.
I won no fame in wearing it, but I
Did not disgrace it, then or now. This prize
I render back to you, with breaking heart.

ALFONSO
You do not see how I feel towards you.

TASSO
My lot is not to think but to obey,
And destiny demands that I renounce
This glorious tribute: crowns do not suit   1570
The heads of prisoners, so let me take
This adornment from my head. I dared to think
This wreath was mine for all eternity,
But that huge happiness was given me
Too early in my life and now, too soon,
It is torn away – I overreached myself.
You take yourself what no one else could take,
And what no god will give a second time.
We mortal beings are most wonderfully
Put to the test, in ways we could not bear   1580
If Nature had not bestowed on us a blessed
Frivolousness of spirit. Necessity
Teaches us to play irresponsibly
With our most priceless possessions. Willingly
We open up our hands, and all those treasures
Vanish beyond recovering. I weep,
And kiss this wreath, and dedicate it now
To transience. This weakness is allowed me . . .
Who would not weep when even immortal things
Are not safe from destruction? Join with this sword   1590
That sadly played no part in winning you,
And twine around it like a wreath of tribute
On the grave of all my hope and happiness!
My lord, I lay them both here at your feet,
For who can be well-armed when you are angry,
Or crowned if he lacks your recognition?
This prisoner goes, to await your judgement.

(Exit. Alfonso signals to a page to carry away wreath and sword.)

SCENE 5

Antonio; Alfonso.

ANTONIO
Where will these ravings lead him? And what are
These lurid colours in which he paints   1600
His talents and his destiny? The young,
For all their inexperience, will believe
They are unique, and chosen – and so therefore
Anything is allowed. This punishment
Will fit the child, and the man will thank us for it.

ALFONSO
I fear that I have punished him too much.

ANTONIO
If you prefer to be lenient, then
Give him his freedom back and let the sword
Settle our quarrel –

ALFONSO
                                  If opinion
Demanded such a course, I might agree.   1610
But tell me first – how *did* you anger him?

ANTONIO
I find it very difficult to fathom.
Perhaps I have injured him as a man
– But as for his noble rank, I gave him no
Offence that I could see. And for all his rage,
Nothing shameful passed *his* lips.

ALFONSO
                                  That is how
Your quarrel looked to me; what I thought

When I came into the room has been confirmed
By all that you have said. When two men quarrel
One reasonably assumes the wiser one   1620
Must be responsible. I insist, therefore,
That you show him no more anger; as things stand,
Surely some guidance would be preferable.
But there is time, and this is certainly
No occasion for a duel. As long as I
Maintain this country's peace, I shall look for peace
In my own house. So I am trusting you
To repair this discord, which you can do
Quite easily. Leonora Sanvitale
Might seek him out and soften him with sweet words;
Then you must go yourself and give him back
His freedom, in my name. Win his trust again,   1630
By speaking nobly and honestly, and do this
As quickly as you can, speaking to him
As a friend would, or a father. I want to hear
That peace has been restored before we leave
– I know you find nothing impossible
If you wish to do it! It is best, I think,
To wait an hour, and then let the ladies
Complete what you have started. When we return,
All trace of this affair will have been erased.   1640
You won't get out of practice, Antonio!
You settle one dispute, then create a new one.
I hope you settle this one just as well.

ANTONIO
I am ashamed. When you speak to me like this,
I see my guilt as if I stood and looked
In the clearest mirror. One easily obeys
A lord who convinces while he commands.

ACT THREE

SCENE 1

Princess, alone.

PRINCESS
What is keeping Leonora? Each moment now
Leaves me more deeply anxious. I hardly know   1650
The truth about what happened, any more
Than I know which one to blame for it . . .
If only she would come! I do not want
To speak to my brother or Antonio
Before I can calm myself – before I know
How things now stand, and what will come of this.

(Enter Leonora.)

SCENE 2

Princess; Leonora.

Leonora! Do you know what happened?
How does it stand between the two of them?

LEONORA
I learned no more than we already knew.
They met and quarrelled, Tasso drew his sword,   1660
And your brother had to part them. It appears
That Tasso started it all; at least,
Antonio has his freedom, and goes round
Conversing with his Prince, while Tasso
Is banished to his room and left alone.

PRINCESS

Antonio provoked him! Tasso is
So quickly hurt if someone treats him coldly.

LEONORA

I think so too. Did you see the cloud
On Antonio's face when he arrived?

PRINCESS

I fear we have forgotten how to listen   1670
To the heart's unspoken messages:
A god within our breast will whisper to us,
Very softly and clearly he will show us
What we should grasp and what we should avoid.
Today Antonio seemed even more
Abrupt than he usually is, and more withdrawn.
When Tasso stood there next to him, my spirit
Warned me to realise the difference:
In face, look, tone of voice, in their whole bearing
These two were opposites! – they could never   1680
Become close friends. But my hopes deceived me:
Were not these two both reasonable men,
Both of them noble and intelligent,
And your own friends? Was there a surer bond
Than the one linking all good men? And so
I urged the young man on, and he gave himself
Entirely – and so warmly – to my wishes!
I should have spoken to Antonio
At once! But I delayed for just a while,
And shrank from immediately pressing   1690
The claims of the young man on him. I relied
On breeding, and on courtesy, on all
That common custom which will interpose
So smoothly even between enemies.
Who would have feared that the experienced man
Would show all the rashness of wild youth?
But it has happened. Evil was far away,
It is upon us. And what are we to do?

LEONORA

How very hard it is to give advice
– You see that for yourself! This is not like   1700
A conflict between like-minded men:
If it were, words and smiles could put it right,
Or if words failed, then weapons. For some time
I've thought that these two men were enemies,
For no more reason than that Nature failed
To make *one* man of them. And had they been
Aware of their interest, they might have joined
As friends together, to go through their lives
With added strength and joy and happiness.   1710
That was my hope – but I see it was in vain.
Whatever caused it, we might easily
Patch up this quarrel; but could we be sure
Of the future, or even tomorrow?
I think it would be best if Tasso left here,
For just a little time: he could make his way
To Rome if he wanted to . . . And Florence . . .
After a few weeks I might meet him there,
And could work on his feelings as a friend.
As for Antonio, this frigid stranger!   1720
Perhaps you would be able then to draw him
Closer to you and your friends. Perhaps
The charitable influence of Time
Will accomplish what seems impossible?

PRINCESS

So you have the pleasure of his company
And I am left without it. How fair is that?

LEONORA

You will not have to give up anything,
Except what you cannot now enjoy.

PRINCESS

Should I cast out a friend so easily?

LEONORA

You would only *appear* to cast him out.   1730

PRINCESS
My brother would not willingly part with him.

LEONORA
When he sees it as we do, he will give way.

PRINCESS
It is hard to condemn oneself to failure.

LEONORA
Why not think of it as rescuing yourself,
And Tasso with you?

PRINCESS
        I shall not consent.

LEONORA
More evil will come of it if you don't.

PRINCESS
You distress me. Are you sure you are doing right?

LEONORA
We shall soon see which one of us is wrong.

PRINCESS
If it must be, then we will talk no further.

LEONORA
Those who make up their minds are freed from sorrow.   1740

PRINCESS
I can't make up my mind . . . Oh then let him go,
If he need not be away for a long time.
We must care for him, Leonora, and make sure
That he lacks for nothing in the future.
I am sure that the Prince will readily
Maintain him, even at a distance.
See Antonio about it, he has

Great influence with my brother, and will not turn
This quarrel to anyone's disadvantage.

LEONORA
One word from you would count for so much more.   1750

PRINCESS
But Leonora, I possess no skill
In pleading for myself and for my friends
In the way my sister might. I lead
A very sheltered life, and gratefully
Accept all that my brother can and will
Provide for me. Once I reproached myself
For doing so; but I have conquered that.
One friend would often scold me about it:
You are unselfish, which is wonderful,   1760
But (she would say) you are *too* unselfish,
You do not fully understand the obvious
Needs of your friends. I could not answer her,
So I had to put up with the reproach;
And so it pleases me the more to know
That I *can* help a friend. My mother left
All her property to me, and I will gladly
Help to provide for Tasso out of that.

LEONORA
And as it happens, I am also able
To show myself a friend. Tasso, we know,   1770
Can't manage things; and where he is in need
I shall certainly know how to help him.

PRINCESS
Take him away, then . . . If I must give him up,
Let it be in your favour. I do see
How that will be the best way. But tell me,
Why must I once again endure a grief
As if it were good, and beneficial?
Ever since I was young I have had to learn

Never to count on any happiness,
So as to feel less sad at losing it.   1780

LEONORA
But I so much hope to see you happy:
Who deserves that more than you?

PRINCESS
                    Leonora –
Happy? Does deserving make us happy?
If only it were true in my brother's case!
His great heart will accept courageously
Whatever fate deals out to him, but does
He gain what he deserves? And is my sister
Happy in Urbino? She is beautiful,
She is gracious and noble; but she has borne
No children to her young husband. He respects her,   1790
And does not make her suffer, but can you see
Any joy in that house? And then what came
Of our mother's intelligence, her knowledge
Of so many things, and her generous mind?
Could it save her from error? They took us
Away from her, she died, and in the end
We knew she was not reconciled with God.

LEONORA
Isn't it best to think of what we have,
And not what we lack? There are so many things
Remaining for you –

PRINCESS
                    There is only one   1800
Thing that remains for me, and that is patience.
I have practised that since I was very young.
When all my friends, my brother, and my sister
Enjoyed themselves at games and festivals,
My illness shut me in my room; from then
I had to learn privation, and how to live
In the company of pain. One of the things

That gave delight in loneliness was the joy
Of singing; so I entertained myself,
Soothing away some of that pain and anguish,
Some of that hopeless longing, with sweet sounds   1810
Which made a pleasure out of suffering,
A harmony from sadness. Yet even this
My doctor soon took away: he ordered me
To lie in a strict silence, live to suffer,
And renounce even that small consolation.

LEONORA
But you found so many friends, and now
You have your health and spirits back again.

PRINCESS
I have my health . . . Or at least I am not sick.
And yes, I have many friends, whose constancy   1820
Makes me happy. And I also had a friend –

LEONORA
Whom you haven't lost!

PRINCESS
                    But I shall lose him soon.
That moment I first saw him meant so much!
I had scarcely recovered from my sufferings,
The pain and the sickness had barely gone:
Shyly and quietly I looked out at life,
Took pleasure in the daylight, recognised
My brother and my sister, even dared
To drink some lovely drafts of hope again.
Then, as I ventured to look further out,   1830
I saw in the distance friendly figures
Coming to meet me – Leonora, what I saw
Was my sister, leading by the hand
A young man whom she introduced to me.
I confess to you – my heart went out to him,
And now it will hold him for ever.

LEONORA

Oh my Princess – you must not regret it.
If you can recognise a noble soul,
You have won something never to be lost.

PRINCESS

Any beautiful and miraculous thing   1840
Is to be feared – like the gentle flame which seems
So gloriously useful while it burns
In our hearth, or lights us from a torch.
Who would want – or could try – to do without it?
But when it eats up everything around it,
How pitiful we are! Please leave me now,
I speak too freely. Even with you I might
Do well to hide how weak and ill I am.

LEONORA

A sickness of the heart may best be cured
By trusting your sorrows to a friend.   1850

PRINCESS

If that is true, then I shall soon be healed.
I give my trust to you, purely and wholly.
And Leonora – I have now decided:
Tasso may go . . . even though I feel it, now,
The long pain of those days when I cannot have
The joy of knowing him. Then the sun
Will no longer lift up from my eyelids
His lovely image as transfigured by
A waking dream; and I shall never rise
With the fond hope of seeing him, my spirit   1860
Yearning for that one moment; my first glance
Into our gardens will be a search in vain
In the dew of the shadows. Wonderfully
Did I have my wish fulfilled, to be with him
On each calm evening. With our friendship came
The desire for a deeper understanding,
A feeling rising higher with each day
Towards the purest harmony . . . But now

The darkness falls before me; the sun's glory,
The happy feeling of a perfect day,   1870
All the varied splendour of the world, is lost
In the mist that surrounds me. Every day
Once seemed a whole lifetime for me. Care and doubt
Were silent, we were happily embarked,
And the stream carried us on the lightest waves
Without our steering. Now all that has gone,
And in this dismal present, a secret
Dread of the future overwhelms my heart.

LEONORA
But the future returns your friends to you,   1880
And brings you new joy and happiness.

PRINCESS
I far prefer to keep what I possess.
Change may divert me, but what use is it?
I was never one to reach down greedily,
With youthful craving, into that urn of fate
Which the unknown world provides – and snatch
Some random toy with which I might console
My hungry and inexperienced heart.
Because I honoured him, I had to love him.
I *had* to love him, since he made my life
More of a life than it had ever been.   1890
At first I told myself, 'Stay well away,'
And I drew back, and back. It brought me closer,
So charmingly enticed, so harshly punished!
A pure, true blessing vanishes from me,
And an evil spirit rewards my desire
With pain instead of joy and happiness.

LEONORA
If the word of a friend cannot console you,
Then the beauty of the world, and time itself,
Will heal your pain without your knowing it.

PRINCESS

I do see that this world is beautiful . . .   1900
Across its surface so much loveliness
Passes before us . . . Why does it always seem
To lie just beyond the reach of human hands,
Tempting our timid longings always forward,
Step by step forward, right up to the grave?
So seldom is it that men find the things
The world seems to promise them, so seldom
Ever retain what once has luckily
Fallen into their grasp. Whatever prize
Yielded itself, it tears itself away;   1910
We clutch it greedily – and let it go.
There is a happiness – we do not know it,
Or if we do, we do not know its value.

(Exit.)

SCENE 3

Leonora alone.

LEONORA

How I do pity her, this noble
And beautiful heart – the sadness of her fate.
But do you hope to gain, then – from her loss?
Is it so necessary he should go?
Or do you want to make it necessary
So that you may possess that heart and talent
For yourself alone? You shared it until now,   1920
Shared it unequally with another.
Are your motives honest? Aren't you rich enough?
What are you lacking? Husband, son, property,
Status, beauty – yes, you have them all.
So do you want to add him to the others?
Do you love him? How explain otherwise
Why you can't do without him? Come, you shall
Admit it to yourself: it is so pleasant

To see yourself portrayed in the clear mirror
Of a poet's mind! Doesn't happiness
Seem greater and more splendid when his poems   1930
Carry us, and exalt us – just as if
We rode the clouds of heaven? Yes,
Only then are you worthy of being envied:
Not only do you have what many crave,
But everybody knows and recognises
What it is you have! Your Fatherland
Speaks of you and looks up to you, you stand
On the highest pinnacle of happiness!
Is Laura, then, to be the only name
On everybody's lips? Did Petrarch have
The only right to give an unknown beauty   1940
An immortal name? And tell me, where is there
A man now living to compare with Tasso?
The world acclaims him, and posterity
Will speak his name with reverence.
How wonderful it is to have him near
In the brightness of this life, and thus
Approach the future with him with light step:
Then time, and age, and shameless rumour sending
The wave of approbation here and there
Can make no difference. Every transient thing   1950
Will live on in his poem; you will remain
Still beautiful and happy even when
The wheel of things has long swept you away.
Yes, you must have him! She will lose nothing,
This is no different from her other passions:
They are like moonlight, wanly shining down
On the traveller's path, never affording
Any warmth, or joy, or pleasure. She herself
Will be pleased to know he is gone, when she knows   1960
That he is happy – almost as pleased
As when she saw him daily. In any case,
I am not banishing us – I shall come back
And bring him with me. Here is Antonio!
I'll see if I can tame our surly friend!

(Enter Antonio.)

SCENE 4

Leonora; Antonio.

LEONORA

I think you brought us war instead of peace!
You might have come straight from a battlefield,
Where violence reigns, and force decides the day,
And not from Rome, where solemn wisdom raises   1970
Hands to bless all the obedience at its feet.

ANTONIO

My beautiful friend! – I do accept the blame,
And yet there is a very good excuse:
If you are striving constantly to be
Wise and judicious, an evil spirit
Lurks at your side and dangerously waits
Its moment to extort a sacrifice.
This time I fear I made my offering
At the expense of all my dearest friends.   1980

LEONORA

You have toiled so long on behalf of strangers
– Accepting *their* opinions – that when you meet
Your friends again, you do not recognise them.
You clash with them, as if they were strangers too.

ANTONIO

Yes, I agree – it can be dangerous.
Living among strangers, you take good care
To stay on your guard; you further your designs
By nurturing their favour, in that way
Making good use of them. Now with your friends
You can relax, and rest in their affection,   1990
And indulge your moods, letting your passions
Have unrestricted freedom: as a result,
The first we hurt are those we love the most.

LEONORA

Now I feel happier. In these reflections
I recognise my friend, the old Antonio.

ANTONIO

I freely admit it: I am annoyed
That I lost my self-control today. And yet,
When a man comes back worn out from all his toil,
And hopes to find some rest in the evening quiet,
In a shady spot, before he hurries on   2000
To his next assignment – if he then finds
The shade pre-empted by some idle chatterer,
Is it not human to react as I did?

LEONORA

If he really is human he will gladly
Offer to share that space with one who makes
His rest more pleasant, and lightens his labour
With conversation on delightful themes.
The tree which gives that shade is a broad tree:
There is space enough for both to rest there.   2010

ANTONIO

And shall we now stop swapping metaphors?
There are quite enough treasures in this world
For some to be shared happily with others.
And yet there is one treasure that a man
Will be happy only to grant to the one
Who truly deserves it, and still another
He never wants to share with any man,
No matter *how* deserving. If you want to know,
One treasure is the laurel, and the other   2020
Is the favour of women.

LEONORA

So now I see!
That wreath of laurel which our young friend wore
Offended this very serious man!
Could you yourself have found a more modest

Reward for his toils, for all his poetry?
His service to us is not of this world:
It hovers in the heavens, filling our minds
With pleasing sounds and gracious images
– So isn't a gracious image a good symbol,
And exactly the prize he should receive?
And if he scarcely ever touches earth,   2030
Then this high prize will scarcely touch his head.
His admirers pay him their barren homage
With a barren branch, an easy discharge
Of their obligation. You would hardly grudge
The golden halo round the martyr's head
In a holy picture? This is the same.
Surely we always see the laurel wreath
– Whoever wears it – as a symbol used
For suffering and not for happiness?

ANTONIO
Are your lovely lips trying to teach me   2040
To disdain the vanities of the world?

LEONORA
I do not need to teach you how to prize
Each possession according to its worth.
But sometimes even a wise man, as much
As others, needs to be shown his possessions
In their true light. You, noble man, would not
Be happy to lay claim to a mere phantom
Of favour and honour. You bind yourself
With a real and living service to your prince,
And your friends are pledged to you in that same way   2050
– So isn't your most suitable reward
Something real and living? Your laurel wreath
Is your prince's unswerving confidence:
It rests on your shoulders as a burden
Which you love, and carry lightly, and your fame
Consists in everybody trusting you.

ANTONIO
Well, what about the favour of women?
You are not saying *that* is unimportant?

LEONORA
Ah, it all depends! You do not lack for it,
But if you did, then you might well survive   2060
– Whereas Tasso could not if he tried.
Can you tell me this: if a woman wanted
To care for you in her own fashion,
Lavishing sundry small attentions on you,
Would she succeed in that? In your existence,
Everything is well-ordered and secure:
You see to your own needs in just the way
You attend to other people's wishes,
And anything which one might like to give you,
You have already. But Tasso needs our help
As women, in our own particular ways.
He always lacks a thousand little things
Which a woman likes to give – for example   2070
Those elaborate clothes he likes to wear,
Those silken cloaks with the embroidery:
He so much loves to see himself well-dressed,
And can't bear even to touch the second-rate
Stuff which a servant wears. All of his clothes
Must be elegant, beautiful and noble,
And he can't find such things for himself.
And he needs our help in keeping what he has:
He is always so poor, so very careless.   2080
On journeys he will leave things everywhere,
Lose half his luggage, or have it stolen
– He has to be looked after the whole time!

ANTONIO
And that pathetic need to be looked after
Makes this youngster more endearing! How lucky
To have one's faults transmuted into virtues,
And be allowed to act the helpless child
On into manhood – yes, even daring

To boast about one's charming weaknesses.   2090
Forgive my sounding bitter, my dear friend
– You leave out such a lot. He is all presumption,
And much more clever than you choose to think.
He prides himself on having two fine flames,
And ties the knots of love this way and that
To enslave their hearts. Can one believe it!

LEONORA

The fact that there *are* two establishes
That none of this is any more than friendship.
But even were we exchanging love for love,   2100
It would still be a very poor reward
For that noble heart, who dreams away his life
In a selfless desire to please his friends.

ANTONIO

So you will go on spoiling him as always,
Interpreting his selfishness as love,
Offending all those friends whose loyal hearts
Are truly devoted to you. Pay this proud man
Your tribute if you wish, but you'll destroy
The bond of trust in this society.

LEONORA

We are not quite so biased as you think.   2110
We take great care to guide him, and correct him,
We aim to educate him to delight
In life all the more, and give to others
More enjoyment for themselves. We are not blind:
We do see things we need to criticise.

ANTONIO

But those are just the things you praise him for!
I have known Tasso for a long time now:
He is easy to know, and far too proud
To conceal his own feelings. There are times
When he sinks down into himself as if
The world were inside him, and he could live   2120

Within that space sufficient to himself.
Then everything around him disappears:
He lets it drop, he lets it go, he pushes
Everything away, hides in himself, and then
– And then! Just as a spark will fire a mine,
He suddenly explodes – with joy, or grief,
Or anger, or caprice, wanting to seize
On everything he can, and hold it fast.
Then whatever he fancies must be done!
Something that should take years must be achieved   2130
Immediately, all those problems overcome
That years of effort could scarcely solve.
He asks the impossible of himself
So as to demand it of others. His mind
Strives for the ultimate in everything
When not one in a million could find it
– And he is not that one. At last, no wiser,
He will draw back inside himself again.

LEONORA

He only hurts himself – not other people.   2140

ANTONIO

Oh no! He frequently does hurt others.
Can you deny that when the passion grips him,
He will abuse and slander his own Prince
And even the Princess – or anyone?
It's true it may be only for a moment,
But that is quite enough; and before long
He begins all over again. He has no
Control over his feelings or his tongue.

LEONORA

I think myself that if he went away,
For a little while, it might be good for him,   2150
And useful for other people also.

ANTONIO

You may be right; and yet it might not help.
However, just now it's unthinkable:
All the blame for it would fall on me,
Since it would obviously appear that I
Had driven him away – which is not the case.
As far as I'm concerned he can stay here,
And if he wants to make it up with me
And follow my advice, then I feel sure
We should be able to get on quite well.   2160

LEONORA

So now you hope to influence a mind
That you seemed to have written off for lost?

ANTONIO

One is always hopeful – and in everything
Hope is a better counsel than despair.
Who knows what might be possible? Tasso
Is dear to our Prince . . . No, he *must* stay here,
And if we fail to educate him – well,
He would not be the only one we'd failed with.

LEONORA

I did not realise you could be so calm
And so unbiased. Suddenly you've changed!   2170

ANTONIO

Middle age can offer one advantage:
You still make appalling blunders, but at least
You recover yourself rather faster!
You want to reconcile me to your friend.
Can I ask you this favour? Would you now
Do what you can to help him find himself,
And bring things back to normal? Very soon
I shall go myself and talk with him – as soon
As you tell me he seems calm; or otherwise

I shall make matters worse! But whatever you do,   2180
Will you do it inside this next hour?
Alfonso still holds to his earlier plan
Of going back tonight; and as you know,
I have to travel with him. Until then . . .

(Exit.)

SCENE 5

Leonora alone.

LEONORA
My dear friend – this time we do not agree!
Our interests do not go hand-in-hand.
In one short hour I need to do my best
To win Tasso over – beginning now!

ACT FOUR

SCENE 1

Tasso, alone.

TASSO
Have you woken from a dream, and has
That beautiful illusion forsaken you?   2190
After a day bright with the highest pleasure
Has sleep subdued you, is your soul now bound
With heavy, tormenting chains of sleep?
Yes, you are awake . . . and you are dreaming.
Where are those hours that played around your head
With wreaths of flowers? And where are the days
When your free spirit, full of longing, rode
The outstretched blue of heaven? You are alive,
You touch yourself; and yet you cannot tell
If you *are* alive. Is it my fault   2200
Or someone else's, that I find myself
Left here like one who is guilty? And is this
A crime I have committed, to suffer so
– Is not my whole mistake a credit to me?
Here is the truth of it: I looked at him,
And was carried away by my goodwill.
My feelings led me into the false hope
That if a man had human features, then
He would be human! I went up to him
With open arms – and I felt locks, and bolts,
Guarding an empty heart. How cleverly
Had I prepared my plan for welcoming   2210
The man I so long felt suspicious of . . .
But whatever happens now, you may hold fast
To this one certainty: I did see her!
She stood there with me, and she spoke to me.

Her eyes, her tone of voice, the words she spoke
– They are mine for ever. Not time, or fate,
Or cruel fortune – none can deprive me
Of gifts like those. And if my spirit soared
Too fast, and if I all too quickly gave   2220
Liberty to that flame which now consumes me,
I shall never regret it, even though
My life's whole fortune were lost for ever.
I pledged myself to her – and gladly followed
Her bidding which led me on to ruin.
Let it be so. At least I showed myself
Deserving of her precious trust, which gives
New life to me – yes, gives me life again
Even in this hour which opens, violently,
The black gates onto an age of mourning.
So, it is done! The sun of my good fortune   2230
Sets, all at once; the Prince withdraws from me
His gracious glances, leaving me to stand
Lost on this narrow path into the dark.
Now they swarm out and beat around my head,
That loathsome retinue of ancient night,
The equivocal and hateful fiends. O where
Shall I go to escape this nausea,
To escape this pit that lies before me?   2240

(Enter Leonora.)

SCENE 2

Leonora; Tasso.

LEONORA
What happened? Dear Tasso, did your own passion
Lead you into this, and your suspicion?
Please, tell me what it was – we are all appalled.
Where was your gentleness and kindly nature,
All that swift insight, and the fine judgement

Allowing you to give each man his due?
Where was your even temper, which suffers
All that good men can bear, but vain men cannot?
Your wise control over what you say?
Oh my dear friend, I scarcely recognise you.   2250

TASSO
And what if all that were now lost?
If you suddenly found out that a rich friend
Had no more possessions than a beggar?
You are right to say it – I am not myself;
And yet I still am just as much myself
As I ever was! It seems a mystery,
And yet it's not. The peaceful moon at night
Irresistibly captures eye and spirit
With its brilliance – then by day it floats along
Like a pale, insignificant little cloud.   2260
I am outshone by the glare of daylight:
You cannot know me now – nor I myself.

LEONORA
My friend, I cannot understand your meaning
When you talk like this. Can you explain yourself?
Has Antonio's blunt insult hurt so much
That now you wholly fail to recognise
Yourself and others? You may confide in me.

TASSO
I am not the one who has been insulted.
You see me punished now because I was
Myself the offender. A sword, of course,
Would quickly slice through any knot of words,   2270
But I am a prisoner. You would not know
– And do not be frightened, my gentle friend –
But this is a prison! The Prince's judgement
Chastises me like a boy – I must obey.

LEONORA
You seem more upset than you need to be.

TASSO

Am I a weak child, then, that you should think
Such an incident would break my spirit?
It does not hurt me deeply, the pain comes   2280
From what it signifies: all my enemies
Can seize their chances, all the envious ones
Have the field entirely to themselves.

LEONORA
                                        Tasso,
These enemies are your own invention,
I'm convinced of it. Not even Antonio
Bears you the least ill-will, however much
You imagine he does. Today's quarrel –

TASSO
Let's leave that entirely aside, let's take
Antonio as he is and always has been.
How he loves to play the master, with a kind   2290
Of pedantic cleverness that riles me!
Instead of trying to establish whether
His listener might not himself be right,
He lectures you on innumerable things
You grasp already, and much more profoundly
Than he does himself. He will not listen,
And prefers to misunderstand you – to be
Misunderstood by one so arrogant,
With his smiles and his superiority!
I am not old enough, or clever enough,
To be patient with such treatment, and smile back.
It would have happened, we were bound to quarrel   2300
Before much longer, and later on
It would have been much worse. I recognise
One master only, he who nurtures me,
No other. I must be free to think and write
– The world restricts our actions as it is!

LEONORA
He often speaks of you with great respect.

TASSO

Don't you really mean 'with great indulgence'?
That is the kind of subtle cleverness
I find unbearable! His talk is so   2310
Glib and equivocal that even his praise
Will sound disparaging. Nothing hurts more
Than bland approval from Antonio.

LEONORA

But you should have heard him for yourself,
Praising the talents that Nature's goodness
Gave you above many others. He does know
What your gift is – and he does value it.

TASSO

Try to believe me: no selfish mind
Can escape the torments of petty envy!
It isn't difficult for such a man   2320
To forgive someone else his wealth, or rank,
Or honours. He can argue to himself:
If you really wanted it, if you persevered
And fortune favoured you, then you yourself
Could have all that. But those most precious gifts
Which only Nature gives, which you can't achieve
Solely through effort, or buy with money,
Or gain by force, or ingenuity,
Or crude determination – *that* kind of gift
He never can forgive. Not envy me?
He who thinks he can, with his pedantries,   2330
Extort the favour of the Muses – reeling off
Quotations from the poets and believing
That makes him one of them? He would far sooner
Grant me the Prince's favour – which he covets! –
Than the gods' gift to a poor orphaned boy.

LEONORA

If only you could see things properly:
You are quite wrong – this is not Antonio.

TASSO

If I am wrong about him, I am glad!
I think of him as my arch-enemy,   2340
And if I had to be more lenient now,
I would be inconsolable. Besides,
It is a folly to be reasonable
In everything – you destroy yourself. Are those
Who oppose us so reasonable? No!
Man has a narrow nature which requires
A twofold quality of love and hate,
In the same way that night must go with day
And sleep with waking. No, from now on,
I must regard Antonio as the object   2350
Of my deepest hatred. Nothing can tear from me
The pleasure of it, all the luxury
Of thinking worse and worse of Antonio!

LEONORA

But Tasso, if you will not change your mind,
I hardly see how you can any longer
Stay at this court. You know how important
Antonio is, and must remain.

TASSO

Oh my dear friend – I know how unimportant
I have been, for a very long time now.

LEONORA

Oh that's not true, nor could it ever be!
Surely you realise just how pleased they are   2360
– The Prince and the Princess – to have you here?
And when Lucretia comes to visit them,
It's as much for your sake as for theirs.
They are full of admiration for you, all
Have an absolute confidence in you.

TASSO

But what kind of confidence is that?
Has the Prince ever granted me one word

About affairs of state? One serious word?
Whenever there was some important question
To discuss with his sister, or with others,   2370
Even when I was there, I was not asked.
The cry would be, 'Antonio is coming!
Write to Antonio! Ask Antonio!'

LEONORA

You are complaining when you should be thankful.
If he likes to leave you altogether free,
That is his way of honouring you.

TASSO

I'm left alone because he thinks me useless.

LEONORA

You are not useless when you are left alone.
You nurse these fears and hatreds in your heart
As if they were delicate children!   2380
Now listen: I have considered all these things,
And whichever way I look at it, I feel
You do not flourish on this lovely ground
Where Fortune has planted you. Oh Tasso –
May I speak plainly? You should go away!

TASSO

Good doctor, you must never spare the patient!
Give him his medicine and never worry
If the taste is bitter. But ask yourself, please,
Whether a cure is possible, my good friend.
I see it all myself – it is all over!   2390
I can indeed forgive him, but he cannot
Forgive me in return. They all need him,
But they do not need me. He is clever,
And sadly I am not. He seeks to harm me,
And I cannot counter him. My friends look on,
And see it differently: they ought to fight,
But they offer no resistance. You believe
That I should go away – well, I do too.

If it must be farewell, I will endure it.
You are parted from me – may I have both   2400
The strength and the courage to part from you.

LEONORA

Everything which confuses us today
Will seem so much clearer at a distance.
Perhaps you then will realise how much love
Surrounded you everywhere; and see
How the wider world is no real substitute
For the true devotion of close friends.

TASSO

That we shall see. But I have known the world
For so long now: the way it casually
Leaves us alone and helpless, and goes its way   2410
Like the sun and the moon and the other gods.

LEONORA

Tasso, please listen: you need never
Go through such torment again. I advise you
To set off first for Florence, where a friend
Will take every care of you – yes, I
Myself am that friend, I travel back
In the next day or so to join my husband.
I know of nothing which would give us two
A greater pleasure than to have you with us.   2420
I believe that you know what kind of prince
Your host will be, what kind of men and women
That beautiful city cherishes . . .
You don't say anything? Well, consider it,
And tell me when you make up your mind.

TASSO

These are wonderful ideas – and secretly,
Exactly what I wished for. But it seems
So new . . . Will you let me think it over?
It should not take me long to decide.

LEONORA

I shall be leaving with the highest hopes   2430
For you, and all of us – and for this house;
And if you think it over carefully,
You will see there is no better answer.

TASSO

Before you go, just one thing – Can you tell me –
What does the Princess think about me now?
Was she angry with me? What did she say?
Did she blame me very much? Tell me the truth.

LEONORA

She knows you well, and so she quite forgave you.

TASSO

Does she think the less of me? No flattery, please.

LEONORA

You don't lose a woman's favour quite so fast.   2440

TASSO

Will she willingly release me, if I go?

LEONORA

If it is for your own good, then yes – she will.

TASSO

But then I shall lose the Prince's favour?

LEONORA

No, he is generous – you can count on that.

TASSO

And does it mean that we leave the Princess
Entirely alone? . . . And even I
Might have meant just a little to her?

LEONORA

A distant friend can still be company
If we know he is happy. We shall succeed!
I shall see you happy – and the Prince commands   2450
That you should not leave here unsatisfied.
Antonio will come and speak with you,
And please – I beg of you – receive him calmly.
He comes in friendship, and he takes the blame
For the bitterness in him which wounded you.

TASSO

I can face Antonio, in every sense.

LEONORA

And if heaven will allow me, my dear friend,
I shall open your eyes before you go:
In this whole Fatherland there is no man
Who hates or persecutes you, no, not one   2460
Who provokes you or does you secret harm.
I think you are so dreadfully mistaken!
Where you once set your mind to work and wrought
For the pleasure of others, this time you have spun
A strange, unhappy web to hurt yourself.
I shall tear that web apart, and put you back
On the path of life again. Come and tell me, soon.

(Exit.)

SCENE 3

Tasso alone.

TASSO

So I am to believe that no one hates me
And no one persecutes me, every trick,
Every web of secret intrigue is my dream!   2470
I have to confess I am in the wrong,
And do injustices to many men

Who don't deserve it of me! All this, too,
When my honour is as clear for all to see
As their own spitefulness! I am to feel
How the Prince approaches me with generous heart,
Raining down favours, heaping gifts on me
In all abundance – while at the same time,
He is still weak enough to let his eyes   2480
Be blinded by my enemies, and his hands
Be tied when they would help me! He cannot see
That they are deceiving him. How can I tell him
That they are all deceivers when I must
Stay silent, and surrender to their wishes
So that they can deceive him quietly,
Deceive him quietly and conveniently?
And who is it giving me this fine advice?
Cleverly wheedling me with shows of charm
And thoughtful good intention? Leonora!
Leonora Sanvitale, my dear friend!   2490
Oh I know you now! Why did I ever
Trust her smooth words? She is not honest.
For all the favour shown, the tenderness,
All the sweet speeches, she has a cunning heart,
And always had. With soft and clever step,
She turns all this to her own sly advantage.
How many times have I not willingly
Deceived myself, even concerning her
– Although it was mere vanity that led me   2500
Astray in the end. Yes! I knew her,
And still I went on flattering myself,
Telling myself, 'Leonora acts like that
With others – but with you it's different,
You are the only one of them to hear
Her true opinions!' Well, I see it now,
Though the knowledge comes too late. She clung
So tenderly to me while I was still
The favourite. Now I am down, she turns
Her back on me, as Fortune does; she comes
As the agent of my enemy, she glides
Like a snake towards me, hissing magic sounds   2510

With the smoothest tongue. Oh she was charming,
More charming than ever, and every word
So reassuring. But no flattery
Could hide her false intention: the plain truth
Stared through the falsehoods written in her face.
If anyone ever tries to find the way
Into my heart without sincerity,
I know at once. I must go to Florence,
As quickly as I can? And why to Florence?   2520
I see precisely why: the Medici
Are newly come to power . . . Well, they are not
Opposed to Ferrara, that is true,
But jealousy can work with a cold hand
To divide the noblest minds. If I obtain
Firm signs of favour from the Medici
– As I might hope to – then the courtiers here
Would question whether I was loyal and grateful,
And my enemies would believe them!
Yes, I'll go away – but not exactly   2530
Where you might want – and farther than you think.
What is left for me here? What holds me back?
Oh now I understand so very well
Each word I drew from Leonora's lips:
Although I could scarcely catch all of it,
Syllable by syllable, now I can tell
What the Princess thinks of me. It is true,
And I must not despair! 'The Princess will
For your own good quite willingly release you.'
If only she felt a passion in her heart   2540
To destroy me, and 'my own good'. I would rather
Death came to take me than this formal hand
Which clasps me, and lets me go. I shall go, then.
Be on your guard, and let no empty shows
Of kindness or friendship mislead you. No one
Can deceive you now – unless it be yourself.

(Enter Antonio.)

SCENE 4

Antonio; Tasso.

ANTONIO
Tasso – I am here to say just one word.
Can you, and will you, listen quietly?

TASSO
You know all action is forbidden me.
It is right for me to wait, and listen.   2550

ANTONIO
I find you in a calm mood, as I hoped,
So I will say it with an open heart:
First, I release you in the Prince's name
From that bond which seemed to imprison you.

TASSO
As a whim bound me, so it sets me free;
But I accept, and will demand no trial.

ANTONIO
Then let me say, on my own part: It would seem
That in my anger certain words I spoke
Hurt you more deeply than I was aware.
Even so, I believe that what I said   2560
Contained no shameful slur upon you.
As a nobleman you need not seek revenge,
And as a man I trust you will forgive me.

TASSO
Which strikes the harder, injury or insult,
I will not now consider. If one pierces
The very marrow, then the other one
Will only scratch the skin. The shaft of insult
Falls on the man who launched it; the well-aimed sword
Will easily satisfy opinion,
But an injured heart takes very long to heal.   2570

ANTONIO

Now it is my turn to beg you, urgently:
Don't withdraw into yourself. Fulfil my wish,
And the wish of the Prince who sent me to you.

TASSO

I know my duty and I will relent.
Let it be forgiven then, so far
As that is possible. The poets tell us
There is a spear which, with a friendly touch,
Can heal the wound it makes. The human tongue
Is blessed with the same property, and I
Shall not maliciously resist it now.   2580

ANTONIO

Thank you. And I would like you now to know
That you may put me and my will to serve you
To the test at once. Tell me how I can be
Of use to you. I will stand by my word.

TASSO

You are offering all that I could want.
You brought me back my freedom; so may I
Ask you to get me the full use of it?

ANTONIO

What can you mean? Will you not tell me clearly?

TASSO

You will know I have finished my poem
– Yet something finished may not be *complete*.   2590
When I handed it to the Prince this morning,
I hoped to ask a favour: down in Rome
Large numbers of my friends have come together,
And some of them have written to me giving
Opinions of many passages. I have found
Some criticisms useful, but there are parts
That still need further work . . . including some
I would not want to change unless my friends

Convince me much more than they so far have.   2600
Not much of this can be resolved in letters . . .
Going to Rome would soon, I feel quite sure,
Help me untie these knots. You see – I meant
To ask the Prince today . . . but lost my chance.
As things stand now I think I hardly dare
Go and trouble him myself. Therefore I hope
That you might gain permission *for* me.

ANTONIO
It does not seem to me advisable
For you to leave here at the very time
When your completed poem brings you praise
From the Prince and Princess. A day of favour
Is like a day of harvest, one should be busy   2610
As soon as it ripens. If you go away,
You may gain nothing, and may even lose
What you have won already. Presence is
A powerful goddess! Think of that – and stay.

TASSO
But what is there to fear? Alfonso
Is noble, and has always shown himself
Most generous towards me. And moreover,
I wish to be indebted to his kindness,
Not influence him by tactics. I would want
Nothing he might repent of giving me.   2620

ANTONIO
Then please don't demand that he release you
Just at this time. He would be most unwilling,
And I almost fear he might not agree.

TASSO
But he would if you asked him properly:
You can do that at any time you like.

ANTONIO
But what sort of reasons should I give him?

TASSO

My poem speaks its own abundant reasons
In every line! What I aspired to write
Deserved some praise, even if the goal
Was beyond my powers. I showed no lack   2630
Of industry or effort: radiant days
And many tranquil nights were given up
To this one sacred task. Humbly I hoped
To show some modest sign of the great gifts
Of the classic masters: I strove ardently
To call our present age from its long sleep
And into noble deeds – and share myself
The risks and glories of a holy war
With a great Christian army. And if my song
Is to arouse the best men in our land,   2640
It must be worthy of them. I owe so much
To Alfonso for what is done, and I would wish
To be further in his debt by completing it.

ANTONIO

But Alfonso is here, in Ferrara,
With others whose advice would be as helpful
As any Roman's. Finish your poem here.
Then, if you like, go and make your name in Rome.

TASSO

Alfonso was the first one to inspire me,
And I shall take my last advice from him.
Then there is your advice, and the advice   2650
Of all the men of judgement at this court
– I esteem it highly. And if, there in Rome,
My friends do not thoroughly convince me
You shall be the final arbiters. And yet,
I must go to see them; because Gonzaga
Has called up a court of judgement for me,
And I should present myself to it, to meet
Flamminio de' Nobili, Angelio
Da Barga, Antoniano, Sperone Speroni
– You know these names! They are men to whom my mind
Submits in deepest trust – and some foreboding!   2660

ANTONIO
You think of yourself alone, and not the Prince.
I am telling you – he will not let you go;
Or if he did allow it, it would be
Only with great reluctance. Please don't try
To demand what he would not wish to give,
Or ask me when I have advised against it.

TASSO
So – when I test the value of your friendship,
You deny me my very first request?

ANTONIO
True friendship shows itself in a refusal   2670
When that is the right way: so often
Love will prove harmful if it merely serves
The wishes of the loved one, and ignores
His happiness. At present you, it seems,
Believe that what you passionately want
Is good for you – and you want it instantly:
A man committing errors will make up
With sheer intensity for all he lacks
In truth and strength. But duty tells me
That I ought to restrain your dangerous haste.   2680

TASSO
For a long time now have I noticed it,
This tyranny imposed by friendship:
Of all the tyrannies it is the most
Unbearable! You see it differently,
And naturally you think your way is right.
I can see that you have my good at heart,
But your way of pursuing it is not mine.

ANTONIO
Then am I to begin by hurting you?
– Fully conscious of the fact, and in cold blood?

TASSO

I will lift that burden from your shoulders.   2690
Nothing you say will ever change my mind:
You have declared me free, and all the doors
Leading towards the Prince are standing open.
The question is: which one of us should see him?
He leaves tonight, so there is little time.
Choose quickly. If you do not go yourself,
Then I will go and risk the consequences.

ANTONIO

But will you not think of postponing it?
Wait till the Prince returns, leave it a while
And forget about today!

TASSO

                              It must be now,   2700
While it is possible! My feet will burn
On this marble floor, my spirit never be
At peace until the dust of the open road
Surrounds me on my journey. Won't you see
How hard it is for me to speak to him?
I cannot hide it: I have no control
Over my actions, and in the whole world
There is no power which has – apart from chains!   2710
Alfonso is no tyrant, he pronounced me
A free man again. How happily
I once would have obeyed his every word
– But today I cannot. Leave me today
In freedom, so that my spirit finds itself.
I shall soon come back to my duty.

ANTONIO

You make me doubtful. What am I to do?
I can see that error is infectious.

TASSO

You want me to believe you wish me well?
Then arrange it all for me, if you can.

If you succeed, the Prince will let me go   2720
And I won't lose his favour or his help.
I shall thank you for that, and gladly rest
In debt to you. But if you harbour
Old grudges in your heart, and try to have me
Banned from this court, with my fortunes blasted,
And driven out helpless into the world,
Then hold to your opinions and oppose me!

ANTONIO
Tasso, since I must harm you anyway,
Then I will choose the path you choose yourself.
Which one of us is right and which is wrong   2730
The outcome will decide. You wish to go.
Before you leave us, I will tell you this:
The very moment you have turned your back
On this great house, your heart will even then
Yearn to come back, though your blind stubbornness
Still drives you forward. Pain and confusion
– Depression also – wait for you in Rome,
And you will fail in what you hope to gain,
Both there and here. And this is not advice,
But a prediction. – You may rely on me   2740
If the worst happens. I shall now find the Prince.

(Exit.)

SCENE 5

Tasso alone.

TASSO
Yes, go . . . Go away and rest assured
That you have convinced me of what you want.
I am learning to dissemble, learning
From a master of the art, and learning
Rapidly. This is the way that life
Compels us to appear like, even to *be*,

The people we were able to despise,
Boldly and proudly. Now I clearly see
How courtly intrigue works: Antonio wants   2750
To drive me away – and yet he doesn't want
To appear to be doing so. Therefore
He plays the kindly man, the clever man,
To leave me weak and foolish: he must be
My guardian, while I turn into the child
Given over to his care – though even he
Can't force me to be the servant. Thus he plans
To cloud the Prince's vision, even obscure
The Princess's understanding! He believes
They should keep me here: though Nature gave me
An abundant talent, she also chose
To mar the gift with various weaknesses: 2760
A sensitive temper, an unbridled pride,
And a mind weighed down with melancholy.
It can't be altered: once Fate forms a man
People have to accept him as he is,
Try to put up with him, and support him
– And then, on some fine, glorious day, perhaps
They will receive a work from him that gives
Delight and joy – an unexpected gain!
In short that man must be allowed   2770
To live and die as he was born. Do I
Still see Alfonso's strong determination
To scorn his enemies, and faithfully
Protect his friends? And do I know this Prince
From the way he behaves towards me now?
Of course I know him! And I recognise
The full extent of my unhappiness . . .
This is my bitter fate, that everyone
Changes towards me, while they will remain
The same to other people – constant, true,
And reliable! With one swift breath
They change, so easily. Antonio's coming
– This single man's arrival – by itself   2780
Has ruined my whole fortune in one hour.
Has he not undermined at its foundations

All my great edifice of happiness?
Must I endure that? Suffer that today?
Yes. Just as everyone came thronging to me,
Now they desert me; just as everyone
Wanted me for himself, now they ignore me.
And why is that? Should Antonio alone
Outweigh my value, all the love they gave   2790
In such abundance? They all fly from me
– Yes, even you, my dearest, my Princess,
You leave me, too. In these dark hours she has not
Sent one sign of favour. Did I deserve it,
This simple heart that worshipped her so freely?
I heard her voice and felt my heart pierced through
With inexpressible longings. When I saw her
The light of day was dimmed, her eyes, her lips   2800
Drew me irresistibly towards her.
My limbs hardly supported me, I needed
Great strength of mind even to keep myself
Upright beside her – not fall at her feet.
I could not drive away that vertigo
– Be strong here, O my heart! And you, clear mind,
Don't let yourself be clouded over now.
Yes – her too! Do I dare to say the words?
I can scarcely believe it, and yet I do
Believe it now, and bitterly desire   2810
To hide it from myself. Her too! her too!
Forgive her utterly, but never, never,
Conceal it from yourself – Her too! Her too!
I ought to doubt this word if one slight breath
Of faith lives in me; but it is engraved
On the brazen tablet of my anguish, like
A decree of Fate! And now my enemies
Are, for the very first time, cruel and strong.
My strength is gone for ever. How can I fight
When she stands in the host against me?   2820
How can I keep my sanity when she
Puts out no hand to help me, turns away
And will not hear my pleading? You have dared
To think of it, and to say it. And it is true,

Before you could have feared it. Now, before
Despair, with brazen claws, tears at your senses,
Let Fate stand trial and hear it: Her too! Her too!

ACT FIVE

A garden.

SCENE 1

Alfonso; Antonio.

ANTONIO
As you suggested, I went back to him   2830
A second time – I have just come away.
I have advised him, urged him – everything! –
And still he will not change his mind. He begs
More ardently than ever that you grant him
Permission for this short stay in Rome.

ALFONSO
This upsets me profoundly, I can tell you!
– And I would rather tell you than have it
Fester inside me. All right, let him go,
Let him launch off on his travels – go to Rome –
I shan't prevent him. But I will not have   2840
Scipio Gonzaga or the Medici
Stealing him from me. We know so well
That all the greatness of our Italy
Comes from the struggles between its princes
To possess and make use of the best people.
A prince without his gathering of talents
Is like a general without an army;
And anyone, whoever he might be,
Who has no sense of the power of poetry
Is a barbarian. I found and chose   2850
Tasso – Tasso is mine – and I am proud
To have him serving me. Seeing that I did
So much to encourage him in the past,
Should I have to lose him without cause?

ANTONIO

I am embarrassed. In your eyes I bear
All the blame for what happened this morning.
I admit my error gladly, and would ask
Your mercy in forgiving me; though if
You still imagined that I hadn't done
All I possibly could to appease him,
I would be inconsolable. Will you   2860
Reassure me, please – so that I may regain
My peace of mind, and my self-confidence?

ALFONSO

Antonio, will you please rest quite assured
That I do not blame you in the least?
I know his mind so well – I realise
How much I have indulged him, and how much
I had forgotten that it was for me
To state *my* wishes. A man can make himself
Master of what he will, and should not let   2870
The pressure of time, or other urgent needs,
Divert him from his intentions.

ANTONIO

When other people help a man so much
Then he should ask himself most carefully
How he might best repay them. Take the man
Who cultivates his mind, steeps himself in learning,
And eagerly devours all the knowledge
That anyone could grasp – that man should feel
Doubly obliged to be master of himself.
Does Tasso ever see it in that light?

ALFONSO

Man was not put on earth to live in peace!   2880
When we think to enjoy ourselves, suddenly
An enemy arrives to test our courage
– Or a friend to test our patience.

ANTONIO
Does he fulfil the elementary duty
Of choosing wisely what he eats and drinks?
Nature has not bound people by the same
Constraints she places on the animals
– Doesn't he rather let himself be tempted
By anything that flatters his palate,
As a child would! When does he ever mix
Water with his wine? Spices, sweet things, spirits,   2890
One after another he gulps them down,
And then complains about his fuddled brain,
Or heated blood, or fits of moodiness,
And blames it on Fate or Nature. Sometimes
I've seen him – bitterly and stupidly
Arguing with his doctor (all of this
Would be ludicrous, of course, if we *could* laugh
At what torments a man and plagues his friends):
'I have these dreadful symptoms,' he will say,
All fraught with anger and anxiety,   2900
'You boast about your skills – then make me better.'
'Well,' says the doctor, 'give up this and that.'
'Oh but I can't!' 'Then try this medicine.'
'Can't stand the taste!' 'Well . . . try just drinking water.'
'*Water*? Are you mad? Water revolts me,
I think I might have rabies.' 'Then I can't help.'
'Why not?' 'Because you'll have new illnesses
One after the other. And though none of this
Will actually kill you, all the same
Your life will be daily misery.'   2910
'Oh fine! So you call yourself a doctor!
If you know what's wrong, you ought to have a cure
– And please make sure that it's a *pleasant* cure,
So I don't have to *suffer* to ease the pain.'
– Oh you may smile, but all of it is true:
You have had all this from him yourself.

ALFONSO
Yes I have, often. And forgiven it.

ANTONIO

Who can doubt that a life of such excess
Gives us wild dreams at night, and in the end
Lands us with nightmares in broad daylight too?   2920
What *are* his suspicions, if not bad dreams?
Wherever he is, he believes himself
Hemmed in by enemies. No one can see
His talent and not be jealous, so everyone
Must hate him, and set out to persecute him.
So he comes running with complaints – forced locks
And intercepted letters – poisoners –
People concealing daggers in their clothes
– All madness! The enquiries you have ordered,
The enquiries you have *made!* Only to find   2930
No sense in any of it. No prince's power
Can ever make him safe, no friend give comfort.
How can you promise peace and happiness
'To such a man? Or even gain pleasure from him?

ALFONSO

You would be right, Antonio, if I saw
Immediate benefit in him for myself.
But I don't – I deem it an advantage
Not to expect such profit as of right.
Servants will work for us in different ways,
And he whose needs are many will employ   2940
Each man according to his skills, and be
Well-served. The Medici teach us that,
So do the Popes: with what indulgence,
What princely patience and what sheer forbearance
Did they support a host of gifted men
Who, as it seemed, required no princely favour,
Yet all the time were much in need of it.

ANTONIO

Who does not know, my lord, that only labour
Teaches us the true worth of what it yields.
Tasso has gained too much from life too soon   2950
To enjoy it wisely. Had he been obliged

To earn what came his way so easily,
He would have used some manly energies,
And known a greater pleasure by proceeding
Step by step, slowly. A poor nobleman
Has gained his life's ambition if a prince
Invites him to serve as his companion
In his own court, and cures his poverty
With a generous allowance. If that prince   2960
Then gives him his full confidence and favour
– Promotes him above others, to assist him
In war, or trade, or earnest conference –
Then, in my view, this modest man should show
A silent gratitude for his good luck.
On top of all this, Tasso has the finest
Success a young man could ever hope for:
His Fatherland has fêted him already,
And looks to his future with high hopes.
Believe me, all this sullen discontent
Rests on a broad pillow of good fortune.   2970
– He is coming now! Release him graciously,
Give him his trip to Rome, or Naples,
Or wherever – what he thinks he misses here
He will find *only* here when he returns.

ALFONSO
Does he want to go back to Ferrara?

ANTONIO
He wants to stay a while in Belriguardo.
Whatever things he most needs for the journey
He will ask someone else to send on.

ALFONSO
Very well, then. My sister and her friend
Return from here tonight; as I am riding,   2980
I shall be home before them. You follow us
When you have taken care of all he needs:
Order whatever may be necessary
From the castellan – so that he may stay here

As long as he wants to, or just as long
As his friends need to help him with his luggage.
I shall be sending him on some letters
To assist him in Rome. He's coming now.

(Exit Antonio. Enter Tasso.)

SCENE 2

Alfonso; Tasso.

TASSO
(with some reserve)
That favour which you have so often shown me
Appears to me today in its full light.   2990
All that I carelessly and wantonly
Did in your presence, you have forgiven;
You reconciled my adversary to me;
You grant me leave now to withdraw myself
For a short time, and are continuing
Your generous favour to me. Thus I leave
With the utmost confidence, in the quiet hope
That this brief interval will bring a cure
For all the stresses that now trouble me:
My spirit shall spring up renewed again,   3000
And on that road where I first happily
Trod with your glance of kind encouragement,
It will prove once more worthy of your favour.

ALFONSO
I wish you all good fortune on your journey,
And hope you will come back a happier man
And completely cured; so that in the end
You will reward us all with twice the pleasure
We lose with each hour you spend away from us.
I have some letters for you – show them please
To my people and friends down in Rome.   3010
Put every trust in them, and realise

That I think of you as mine, even though
You may be briefly absent from my court.

TASSO

O Prince, you overwhelm with favours one
Who considers himself unworthy . . .
For the moment, I cannot thank you.
Therefore, instead of thanks, may I put to you
One small request? You realise that my poem
Is very precious to me: I have worked hard,
And spared no care and effort; but even so   3020
There is still a good deal left for me to do.
In Rome, where the spirits of the great still throng
In the minds of living men, I wish once more
To go to school, and bring you back a poem
More justly deserving of your applause.
Will you please return me those manuscripts
I left with you . . . I am ashamed of them.

ALFONSO

Are you really wanting to snatch away
The gift you have only just brought me?
– Let me step in to arbitrate between   3030
You and your poem: You should take special care
Not to spoil its lovely living freshness
By reworking it too much, and seeking
Advice from all and sundry. The poet
Shows his true skill by cleverly uniting
A thousand thoughts contending in the minds
Of a multitude, of all shades of opinion.
Many of them he will not please at all,
But that will not deter him – that will mean
He delights some others all the more.   3040
Now – I don't say you should not try to make
Some modest improvements here and there,
So I promise you – you will have a copy, soon;
Though I will keep your fine original
So that I may enjoy it first myself,
Together with my sisters. Later on,

If you can bring me something even better,
We shall then feel an even greater pleasure
– And only criticise it, if at all,
In a spirit of genuine friendship.   3050

TASSO

May I, my lord – I am ashamed to ask –
Repeat my request? Let me have the copy
As quickly as you can. My mind is on it,
Now I must make it all that it can be.

ALFONSO

I feel your impulse is most praiseworthy.
But, my dear Tasso, surely you should first
Go and enjoy your freedom for a while?
Relax a little; go off and take a cure
To cleanse your blood. That way, the noble
Harmony of your senses will be restored,   3060
Granting you everything that now, in vain,
You seek to accomplish through painful toil.

TASSO

That might seem so, my Prince. But I am well
Only when I am given up to my work.
Only my writing – nothing else – can cure me.
You have been long aware how bad it is
For me to spend my time in luxury
– And least of all does 'peace' mean peace of mind!
I sense that Nature did not wish this spirit
To float at ease on the soft element   3070
Of each calm day – and down into Time's wide sea.

ALFONSO

All of your thoughts and actions lead you
More deeply into yourself! Around us lie
The many pits that Fate has dug for us,
But the deepest is here in our own hearts,
And how tempting it is to leap in.
I beg you – seek some respite from yourself:
The man will gain what the poet loses.

TASSO
This impulse is not to be resisted:
By day and night alike it rules my being,   3080
And if I did not write, and think, poetry,
My life could not have the name of life.
You may as well forbid the silkworm spinning,
Though it is spinning nearer and nearer death,
Drawing out all the time from its inmost self
The precious web, never at rest until
It has sealed itself in its own coffin.
If only some god would grant to us
That creature's enviable fate: one day
To rise on swift and joyful wings, and fly   3090
In some new valley of the sun.

ALFONSO
                                    Please – listen.
The pleasure many people gain from life
Is twice as much for what you give them.
I beg you – see the value of the life
You still possess, with its tenfold riches.
So – farewell! We shall welcome you
All the more warmly if you come back soon.

(Exit Alfonso.)

SCENE 3

Tasso alone.

TASSO
O heart, be firm. It was right that way.
How difficult it is for you, this first
Time you have ever wanted to deceive   3100
And *could* deceive. How easily you knew
That those were not his thoughts, and not his words.
It seemed to me I heard Antonio's voice
Sound out all over again. Therefore

Be careful now; because from this time on
You will hear it so strongly on all sides.
Be firm: you must deceive a little longer,
The man who learns deception late in life
Has honesty to help him. It *will* work,
If you only practise it with them.

(After a pause.)

But you boast too soon . . . She is coming now,   3110
The gracious Princess . . . How can I –?
Now she comes, and my anger and suspicion
Dissolve into grief in my heart . . .

(Enter Princess.)

SCENE 4

Princess, Tasso. Towards the end, the others enter.

PRINCESS
Is it true, Tasso, that you mean to leave us?
Or is it rather that you would prefer
To remain in Belriguardo – and leave later?
I hope you only want to go to Rome
For a little while?

TASSO
                    I'll go there first of all,
And if my Roman friends receive me kindly   3120
– As I dare hope they will – then I perhaps
May work, with care and patience, to make some last
Improvements to my poem. Gathered in Rome
Are talents in profusion, and they all
Are living masters in the various arts.
In that first city of the civilised world,
Does not each corner speak to us – each stone?
How many thousand silent mentors there
Call out to us in friendship, stir our minds

With solemn majesty! So, if my poem
Is not finished there, then I will never
Complete it anywhere. But oh, I feel   3130
My luck is doomed with any undertaking . . .
I may alter things, but never finish it,
And art, which carries life to everyone
And feeds the healthy spirit, will destroy me,
And drive me away. I must leave quickly – now –
I'll go to Naples!

PRINCESS
But do you dare?
Naples once banned your father, and you too,
And the order has never been rescinded.

TASSO
You are right to warn me; I have thought of that.   3140
I shall go disguised, in a pilgrim's clothes,
Or dressed as a shepherd. No one will see me
As I steal through the town, those teeming thousands
Easily hide one man . . . Now I hurry
To the shore, where I find myself a boat
Full of kind, willing people, peasant farmers
Going home from market, people from Sorrento . . .
I must hurry over to Sorrento.
My sister lives there still – she and I   3150
Were my parents' only joy in all their grief.
I am silent on the water, silent yet
As I step ashore . . . Slowly I walk
The path uphill, and at the gate I ask
'Where does Cornelia live? Cornelia
Sersale?' A friendly woman at her wheel
Points out the street to me, shows me the house . . .
As I climb farther, children run beside me,
Staring at my wild hair and wondering at   3160
The melancholy stranger . . . Suddenly
I am at her threshold, and already
The door stands open . . . So I step inside –

PRINCESS

Oh Tasso – if you can, look up at me.
Can't you recognise the danger you are in?
I spare your feelings, or I would be saying –
Is it noble to speak as you are doing?
Is it noble to think only of yourself,
As if you were not hurting your friends?
Are you so unaware of what my brother
Thinks of you? How Lucretia and myself   3170
So cherish you? Can you not feel all this,
And recognise it? Why should it all have changed
In a few moments? If you want to go,
Must you leave us in anxiety and pain?

(Tasso turns away.)

How comforting it is to make some small gift
To a friend who will be going away,
If only a new cloak, or a new sword.
But what else can you have when you reject
All the things you possess, and choose to take   3180
The pilgrim's shell, the smock, and the long staff
For a life of willing poverty?
You take away those very special pleasures
You can only enjoy by being with us.

TASSO

Then you don't want to banish me completely?
Oh these are precious words, sweet comfort to me!
Plead for me, will you! . . . Give me your protection.
Let me stay in Belriguardo; or send me
Over to Consandoli – anywhere!
The Prince has so many fine palaces,   3190
So many gardens which will need attention
All the year round, though you scarcely ever
Set foot in them, even for one short day
– Even one hour! Yes, choose for me the one
– The very farthest – which you do not visit
For years on end, lying uncared for now,
And send me there! And there let me be yours,

Tending the woodlands, covering the lemon-trees
With boards and tiles in the autumn, keeping them
Safe under their thatch of woven reeds.　　　　3200
The loveliest flowers shall take root in that soil,
Every path, and every plot of land
Shall be bright and clean. Let me look after
The palace too! At the right time of year
I will open the windows so as to keep
The paintings safe from damp, and I will clean
The beautifully-decorated walls for you,
Brushing the dust away *so* softly.
The floors will shine out, clean and brightly-polished,
No stone or tile shall be out of place,　　　　3210
And no weed shall sprout in any crack!

PRINCESS

I can find no advice in my heart,
And no consolation for you or – us.
My eye casts round in case there is some god
Who might take pity on us, offering
Some healing herb, or medicine, to bring
Some peace to your mind, and peace to us.
The truest word that lips could ever speak,
The finest remedy – these will not work now.
So I must let you go, and yet my heart　　　　3220
Cannot leave you.

TASSO

So – is it really her?
Does she speak with you, and pity you?
And did you not misjudge this noble heart?
Was it possible that, even in her presence,
Despair took hold of you, and overwhelmed you?
No – it is you – and now I am myself!
Oh please go on speaking, and let me hear
Each word of consolation you can speak.
Don't hold back your advice – what shall I do?
How might I ask your brother to forgive me?　　　　3230
How might I ask you to forgive me too?

So that you all are happy, as before,
To count me as your own? Please tell me that.

PRINCESS

Tasso, what we are asking is so little
– And yet it still seems to be all too much:
You should yield yourself to us as a friend.
We don't want anything you cannot be,
If you would only try to be content
With yourself. That is *our* happiness,
And you upset us only when you shun it.   3240
If we become impatient, that is only
Because we want to help you, which we cannot,
Unless you will endeavour to reach out
And grasp the hand of friendship we have offered
So many times – sincerely but in vain.

TASSO

It is you yourself, come like an angel
As on that first day of all. Oh forgive
The mortal's clouded vision, he did not
Know you at once – but he does know you now!   3250
His soul is once again completely open
To worship you for ever, and his heart
Is full to the brim with tenderness.
It is her . . . She stands here with me . . . What a feeling!
Is it distraction that draws me to you?
Or madness even? Or do I have some rare
Awareness that for the first time now
Helps me to grasp the highest, purest truth?
Yes – this is the one feeling that can make me
Happy on earth, that brought me misery
When I resisted it, and even wanted   3260
To banish it from my heart. I fought with it,
I disputed and disputed constantly
With my inmost being, and shamelessly destroyed
That self to whom you utterly belong.

PRINCESS
If you want me to hear you out, Tasso,
Then moderate this passion – it alarms me –

TASSO
Will the rim of the glass contain the wine
That foams – and seethes – and overflows?
With every word you increase my happiness,
With every word your eyes shine more brightly.   3270
I feel myself transformed, I feel myself
Unburdened of all misery, and free
As a god is free! And you have done all this.
An indescribable power controls me,
It flows from your lips, and yes, it makes me
Your own completely, for all of the future
Nothing more of my self will belong to me:
My eyes are blind with light and happiness,
My senses fail, I am too weak to stand –
You draw me to you – I cannot resist –   3280
My heart goes out towards you, it cannot stop –
You have won me for ever – my whole being –
(He falls into her arms and presses her to him.)

PRINCESS
(pushing him away from her and hurrying away)
Away from me!

LEONORA
(who has shown herself in the background for a short time already.
She hurries forward.)
What has happened? Tasso! Tasso!

(She goes after the Princess.)

TASSO
(about to follow them)
Oh God!

ALFONSO
(who for some while has been drawing near with
Antonio)
He is going mad! Take hold of him!

(Exit.)

SCENE 5

Tasso; Antonio.

ANTONIO
If some enemy of yours were standing here
To see you now – one of those enemies
You always think you see surrounding you,
How he would gloat! Unhappy man,
I can hardly believe what I just saw!
When something shocking or appalling happens,   3290
Our minds are frozen for that instant;
We have nothing with which we can compare it.

TASSO
(after a long pause)
I see it is you. Carry out your duty.
You certainly deserve the trust of princes.
Do your duty, and torture me to death
Since I stand condemned. Take hold, and pull
On the arrow in my side, draw on it hard
So that I feel the barb which fiercely tears
The flesh apart. You serve a tyranny: 3300
You can be its gaoler and its torturer,
Both tasks will suit you very well indeed.

(Looking offstage.)

Yes go, you tyrant, with your victory.
You could not deceive to the very end.
This is your slave and you have chained him well,
Saved him up well for all the torments

You carefully prepared. Go – I hate you,
I loathe the power of tyranny, which seizes
And holds all the world in its wanton grasp.   3310

(After a pause.)

And am I now to be banished utterly,
Banished from here and cast out like a beggar?
Was that why they crowned me – to lead me out
Dressed up like a beast and meekly brought
To the altar of sacrifice? Even today,
On this last day, they lured away from me
– With such smooth words! – my only property,
My poem – and held on to it so tightly.
My only possession is in your hands,
The work that would have recommended me
In every place, the one thing left to me
To keep me from starvation! Now I see   3320
Why he said 'Enjoy your freedom': conspiracy
Was closing round me, and you were its leader.
So that my poem should not be completed,
So that my name should not be known abroad,
So that my bitter rivals might detect
A thousand blemishes – so that in the end
All memory of Tasso might be wiped
From the minds of men – that was the plan they had!
And so I must get used to idleness,
I must preserve my lovely peace of mind . . .
O worthy friendship, kind solicitude!
How I detested it, that unseen, cold   3330
Conspiracy which subtly formed around me
– How much more hateful has it now become!
And you, the siren, tenderly tempting me,
I understand you now – But why so late!
So willingly do we deceive ourselves,
Honour the dross which seems to honour us!
Men have no understanding of each other.
Only galley-slaves – gasping for breath,
All tightly chained together, on one bench   3340
Where no one has any claims to make

And no one has a single thing to lose
– They understand each other! Each one knows
He is no better than a criminal
In a world of criminals. Yet with us,
How blandly will men of taste and manners
Mistake their fellows, just so that others
Mistake them in return! So – all that time
Your saintly outward features hid from me
The tactics of the whore! Now the mask falls,
I see Armida – and her painted charms
Are shrivelled away! Yes, it is you   3350
I wrote about – and I foretold it all!
And the other one, the cunning go-between,
I understand her too, and I despise her.
I hear her soft tread as she rustles round me
In cunning circles. Yes, I know you all,
And let that be enough! I shall praise misery
For robbing me of all things but the truth.

ANTONIO

I am astonished as I listen to you,
Even though I know how your wild spirit   3360
Can waver between extremes. Now calm yourself,
And try to check your rage. These are blasphemies!
In your wild anguish you are saying things
Other people will excuse you, but which you
May never forgive yourself for saying.

TASSO

Don't speak to me in that bland way of yours!
I have no wish to hear your prudent thoughts.
Leave me this hollow happiness, so that
I may rage on into madness: I am
Destroyed inside myself, and living on   3370
Only to feel the agony of that.
Despair in all its fury seizes me,
And in this hell of torment, blasphemy
Is the least cry of pain. I will go away.
If you are honest, show it – let me leave now.

ANTONIO

I will not leave you in such wretchedness;
And if your self-control has broken down,
I promise you, my patience will not fail me.

TASSO

I must surrender? Yes, it is over now,   3380
The best way is to offer no resistance.
So I will only say again, in sorrow,
That what was given me was beautiful,
And I have cast it foolishly away.
They are leaving . . . Oh God, I see already
The dust raised by their carriage-wheels, the riders
Going ahead of them . . . There they go, now . . .
They are lost in the distance . . . Didn't I
Arrive on that road? They are angry with me . . .
If only I could kiss his hand once more.   3390
If only I could say once more, 'Farewell,
Forgive me!' – and then hear him say once more
'It is forgiven you.' – But I don't hear it,
And I will never hear it. Yes, I will go,
Let me just take my leave and go from here.
Give me, oh give me back the present
For one short moment. Then perhaps I might
Recover again. But no, I am cast out,
I am cast out and banished, banished
By myself alone, no longer shall I hear   3400
This voice, or see this glance, no longer –

ANTONIO

If you can heed my voice, the voice of one
Who has some compassion for you, let me say
You are not so wretched as you believe.
Be calm. You give in to yourself too much.

TASSO

Am I as wretched, then, as I appear?
Am I as weak as I now seem to you?
Is everything then lost? And has the pain,

Like an earthquake, brought the whole building down 3410
In pitiful ruins? And therefore have I
No talent left, which might divert my mind
In a thousand ways, and support my spirits?
Is all the strength that once stirred in my heart
Extinguished, utterly? And have I become
A nothing, an absolute nothing?
No – it is all there still – and I am *nothing*.
I am wrenched from myself, and she from me!

ANTONIO

Though you feel you have lost yourself completely,
You can try to recognise what you are!   3420

TASSO

Yes – you remind me at the proper time.
Will history not give me an example?
Is there no noble man who has suffered more
Than I have suffered – one who might stand here
So that I could compare myself with him
And quiet my misery? No, all is lost.
Only this remains: that Nature gives us tears,
The cry of suffering, when finally
Man cannot bear the pain. And me she gave,
Above all, word and melody for grief,   3430
So as to tell the depths of my distress:
Where other men must suffer grief in silence,
A god gave me the power to speak my pain.

(Antonio steps towards him and takes him by the hand.)

O noble man, you stand there firm and quiet,
I seem to be only the storm-tossed wave.
But consider this, and do not presume
Too much on your great strength: for Nature,
Who set this rock in place, has also given
A power of ceaseless movement to the wave.
She sends her tempest and the wave draws back,   3440
Rears itself up, and seethes, and overturns
In bursts of outflung spray. Yet this same wave

Once held the sun, so calmly; and all the stars
Once rested on its gently stirring breast.
The splendour vanishes, the peace is fled.
In this danger I no longer know myself,
And I feel no shame in confessing it.
The helm is broken, and on every side
The ship is cracking. Under my feet
Its deck is splitting now, rending apart.   3450
I reach out to you with open arms,
Just as the sailor clings fast to that very
Rock upon which his vessel should have foundered.

NOTES

It is the purpose of these notes to elucidate some references to the life of the historical Tasso and the d'Este family, not to comment on the text. Grateful acknowledgement is made to Basil Blackwell Ltd, Oxford for their kind permission to make use of some notes in *Goethe's Torquato Tasso* (the German text), edited by E. L. Stahl (1962).

The scene: The palace of Belriguardo. Belriguardo was situated some six miles south-east of Ferrara. It had been greatly enlarged and enriched by Alfonso's father, Duke Ercole II.

Lines 67-68: *Ippolito d'Este,/And Ercole d'Este!* Uncle and father respectively of Alfonso II and Leonora; the brothers were munificent patrons of the arts.

Line 102: *your sister.* Leonora's sister Lucretia had married the Prince (later Duke) of Urbino. See also lines 889-90.

Line 354: *Consandoli.* A villa owned by Alfonso a few miles from Belriguardo.

Line 411: *the plight of my dear parents.* Tasso's father had fled the country after a quarrel with his patron, leaving his wife with Torquato Tasso and his sister Cornelia in penury in Sorrento.

Lines 603-4: *Gregory/– The worthiest ever to wear his crown.* Relations between Ferrara and the Papacy had been less than cordial earlier in the century; in 1521 Papal forces had advanced to within twelve miles of Ferrara.

Line 1563: *the cardinal.* Cardinal Luigi d'Este, brother of Alfonso II.

Line 1795: *error.* The mother of the Princess and Alfonso was a supporter of Calvin, who once came to preach at her court in Ferrara, and her religion cost her her marriage to Ercole II.

Lines 2094-96: *He prides himself . . . Can one believe it!* A close translation from a sonnet on Tasso by his rival the Ferrara poet Battista Guarini, quoted by Serassi:

> 'Di due fiamme si vanta, e stringe e spezza
> Più volte un nodo; e con quest' arti piega
> (Chi'l crederebbe!) a suo favore i Dei . . .'

Line 2422: *Your host*. Francesco I de' Medici, who ruled in Florence from 1564 to 1587.

Line 3181: *The pilgrim's shell*. It was the custom for pilgrims returning from the Holy Land to decorate their hats with shells.

Line 3322: *you were its leader*. Tasso is thinking of Alfonso, not addressing Antonio.

Lines 3349-50: *Armida . . . shrivelled away!* In Canto 18 of *Jerusalem Delivered* the enchantress Armida turns into a hideous monster.

FURTHER READING

The literature on Goethe in English normally quotes him in the original. But the reader with no German who is prepared to trace quoted passages by the line-numbers to the text of the present translation can still take pleasure and profit from, in particular, two essays. Elizabeth M. Wilkinson, 'Goethe's *Torquato Tasso*. The Tragedy of the Poet', in E. M. W. and L. A. Willoughby, *Goethe, Poet and Thinker* (London, 1962) argues that key speeches in the play show Tasso in the act of poetic composition. Ronald Peacock's book *Goethe's Major Plays* (Manchester, 1959) has a chapter on *Torquato Tasso* which presents a judgement on the poet and his relations with the court diametrically opposed to the one offered in my Introduction. Interestingly if belatedly, I find that the German director Peter Stein's stage production of *Tasso* (Bochum, 1969), bizarre excrescences apart, followed a similar line to my own: see Michael Patterson, *Peter Stein* (Cambridge, 1982), chapter 2.

For the social and literary background of Goethe's work, with a detailed account of the Weimar court and the culture that surrounded it, see W. H. Bruford, *Culture and Society in Classical Weimar* (Cambridge, 1962). A broad picture of Goethe's work in a German and European literary and historical context is attempted in my book *The Classical Centre: Goethe and Weimar 1775-1832* (London, 1980). For a concise presentation of Goethe's life and work aimed at the general reader (with all quotations in English), see my volume *Goethe* in the Oxford University Press's series Past Masters, 1984.

T. J. Reed